Also by Dotson Rader

I Ain't Marchin' Anymore!
Government Inspected Meat and Other Fun
   Summer Things

BLOOD
DUES

DOTSON
RADER

BLOOD DUES

ALFRED A. KNOPF
NEW YORK
1973

THIS IS A BORZOI BOOK
PUBLISHED BY ALFRED A. KNOPF, INC.

Portions of this book have appeared in *Partisan
Review, Esquire,* and *Evergreen Review.*
Lines from "For a Young Widow" are from *Homespun
of Oatmeal Gray,* by Paul Goodman. Copyright © 1969,
1970 by Paul Goodman. Reprinted by permission of
Random House, Inc. Lines from "What Were They
Like?" are from *The Sorrow Dance,* by Denise
Levertov. Copyright © 1966 by Denise Levertov
Goodman. Reprinted by permission of New Directions
Publishing Corporation. "Fire in the Architecture
Institute," *Antiworlds and the Fifth Ace,* by Andrei
Voznesenski. Copyright © 1963 by Encounter Ltd.,
© 1966, 1967 by Basic Books, Inc. "American Pie" by
Don McLean. Copyright © 1971, 1972 by Mayday Music,
Inc. and Yahweh Tunes, Inc. All rights administered by
Unart Music Corporation, New York. Reprinted by
permission of Unart Music Corporation, New York, N.Y.

Library of Congress Cataloging in Publication Data
Rader, Dotson.   Blood dues.
    1. Radicalism—United States.   2. Young adults—
United States—Political activity.   I. Title.
HN90.R3R3   322.4'2   73–7279
ISBN 0–394–48274–3

Manufactured in the United States of America
FIRST EDITION

For Ruth Ford

Life is a series of burned-out sites.
Nobody escapes the bonfire:
if you live—you burn.

*BLOOD
DUES*

It was during the Cuban Missile Crisis in 1962 that I first considered myself a leftist. I come from a very conservative family. My rejection of my parents' rightist politics was therefore a dramatic, indeed traumatic, change in my life. The Cuban Missile Crisis frightened me. My terror was quite understandable considering that for a time it appeared that the world was poised at the brink of Armageddon. I became a pacifist and joined the Student Peace Union and actively protested against the threat of war. This was before Vietnam became a large issue in American life. Rather rapidly, in less than a year's time, I moved left, away from pacifism, to embrace what can be termed a radical democratic-socialist position. In other words, on the questions of imperialism and war, capitalism and racism, I took a strongly socialist-oppositionist position. Through the decade of the sixties I was more or less continuously active on the left and I participated in most of the major events of the New Left and antiwar movements during those years.

Recently, however, in the last year or so, something confusing has happened to me. Disillusionment, a fatigue coupled with anxiety without apparent motive, a sense of failure before life. I don't mean simply personal failure. It is worse than that. I mean failure of ideas and imagination and collective action. The failure of a movement. It isn't that the failure is recent. No, only my conscious-

preface

*ness of it is new. Slow in many things, I was late in under-
standing that something had shifted in history, and it was
now being reflected in my life.*

*If I were to place an exact date on that shift in history, the
precise moment at which luck turned or I did or my courage
did not hold, when things began to crumble, crack, not quite
make sense to me, when it did not work anymore, that date
would be the first week in July 1969. The place would be the
Coliseum in Chicago and the occasion the last national convention of the Students for a Democratic Society (SDS).*

*If we are to understand the years that followed and, in the
instance of this book, what happened to me and some of my
friends on the left, and my later involvement with Mailer
and Tennessee Williams and the rest and the disillusionment which came on their heels, it is helpful to know something of the beginning of the breakup. It began, or rather
took its initial form, in Chicago at the last congress of the
student left. I am going to tell you about that event as a
background to what comes later in this book.*

*The last SDS convention was the watershed of the student
left movement, the point at which its decline became irrevo-
cable insofar as it touched the lives of many young Americans. From around the time I became a national member
(1965) until its collapse four years later SDS was the most
important element in the broad coalition of leftist forces
known as "the movement." It was the largest and most influential student left organization ever to exist in the United
States. It is fair to say that in the creation of SDS, in its
founding at Port Huron in 1962, were planted the seeds of
energy and imagination and revolt of the New Left. So when
SDS died in 1969 the central trunk of the young left movement shattered and split, its branches fell.*

*It did not have to end as it did, unless collectively and
mystically its members' weaknesses, their opportunism and
youth and careerist ambitions and romanticism and taste
for power, conspired there to join the disparate political
tendencies toward unreason in the movement to bring it*

down. In retrospect the collapse itself was remarkable, a mystery, for gathered there was almost all of the organizational genius of the New Left which had weaved and pivoted through the last decade, from the Pentagon terraces to the Chicago parks, leaving the country baffled and anxious in its wake. At the SDS convention, and later in the Weatherman "Days of Rage," something ended in history or veered to the right away from us, away from history as I believed it would inevitably be. And this turning occurred then, at the close of the sixties. What happened? Why, to teeter on the edge of self-pity, did we seemingly put out so much and receive so little in return?

Five of us left Boston for Chicago at 6 A.M. on the last Monday in June 1969. We drove straight to Chicago, never stopping to sleep, avoiding the Canadian border because of customs and the threat of false arrest; avoiding the cities and the towns of the Middle West where I had grown up, because they too seemed infested by police . . . and our license plates were out of state everywhere but Massachusetts, Jim's hair too long, and we looked altogether too funkyradical smartassed punk. This was a year after the murders of King and Bobby Kennedy, after the Chicago convention and the abdication of Johnson and the election of Nixon. So we were paranoid out of the East and went straight through to Chicago, avoiding the people.

On the road Eric Mann and three young men (radical students from Boston) and I talked about the movement in the United States, which we were very optimistic about, and how it was somehow going to translate European and Asian revolutionary experience into American terms.

In many ways Eric Mann's experience read like a history of the movement, for he had early organized boycotts against segregation in the South, had started the first teach-ins in Washington against the war. He had worked with Tom Hayden (a cofounder of SDS) in creating the Newark Community Union Project, the first major attempt by SDS to organize an off-campus constituency, and since 1967 had been SDS organizer at Boston University and a member of its national council.

We talked ideology. Nineteen sixty-nine was the Year of the Ideologue in the history of the New Left, and even before we arrived at the SDS convention, we knew the division in our ranks was an ideological one between Progressive Labor (PL) and the SDS National Office, each assuming different and contradictory positions on the main questions entertained by the movement. I did not believe that ideological struggle could wreck SDS, as it had once bitterly divided and broken the Communist party. Even though I was one of the troops, far from any pretense to leadership, I felt we had all been through too much in the past decade to permit our solidarity to die over ideological disagreements that I did not fully understand.

In the car we sang. Because most of us had passed somewhere a civil rights romance (my very first left-wing political act was to picket Woolworth's to protest segregation in their Southern outlets—1962), we sang, somewhat self-consciously to be sure, the integrationist standards, "We Shall Not Be Moved," "Before I'll Be a Slave" . . . Mississippi summer in the car, going back.

And then, because the movement by 1969 had developed from left-liberalism to radicalism to a revolutionary consciousness, because some of us had discovered recently we were Marxists or at least affected Marxist rhetoric, we sang, I for the first time, "Arise ye prisoners of starvation . . ." unconscious of the irony of singing the "Internationale" in a car full of young men like myself, middle-class college students and recent graduates, part of the middling privileged ranks of the United States, singing it and drinking beer like fraternity brothers barreling home from a football game and feeling triumphant and self-dramatic, and wanting revolution (the many meanings of that word!), for in the desire was magic enough.

"Revolution." I used the word enough, applied it to myself when the application was absurd. Now it is difficult to speak it without self-consciousness, the sense of falling short. In 1969 it was different. I suppose because I was younger then and did not know my limits and could think of myself, certainly falsely, as separated from and cleaner and more righteous than my parents' generation. And yet I was honestly moved by concern for the world, for the suffering of people. Revolution was a word filled with remedy, potent and erect and bringing to my mind pictures of revolutionaries storming the White House. How easy it was. Without the drama of revolution I could envision no future to match the excitement of my youth.

The "drama of revolution." The phrase itself gives me away. I visualized revolutionaries romantically, perhaps unseriously, as a band of knights-errant, guerrillas, a gang of bikeboys roaring through the streets. I do not think I was alone in that, because when the Weatherman established itself, it was the motorcyclist's uniform it adopted as its own. Revolutionary/bikeboy: it was that figure which played, like the cowboy, a peculiar and major role in my imagination. And that was very American, my mind bent that way by movies and television and bad novels and the experience of growing up in America. Even the literature of revolt was colored by this romantic sensibility: revolutionary figures, many bloody, there to emulate, martyrs pasting glamour onto death. We were stuffed with martyrs. Live like Che! The dead embraced the living. It was through the romantic marriage of sex and violence and politics and manhood and death that I came to understand how so much of what was apparently apolitical in American culture was indeed revolutionary: drugs, perverse sex, even Warhol's hustler movies, on and on.

Revolutionaries and bikeboys and other tough outsiders were rebel figures to me; the butch stance, the ruthlessness, the overstated masculinity, the power of their bodies and their machines, the independence and mobility evidenced by their lives, their position as outlaw, all constituted their appeal. Che darting through the forest with his men. Scorpio Rising.

In America this sexual-political construct had to be leftist, since its appeal was a compensatory one, contingent upon feelings of powerlessness. Those feelings mandated that the enemy against which these romantic figures acted be the State, the oppressor, the established and the powerful. I could identify with revolutionaries liquidating a ruling class, or with a band of bikers terrorizing the straight countryside. I could identify with violence pitted against established order.

Of course, the attractiveness of this image of violence and my insistence on giving it political content were based upon sexual disorder, feelings of sexual inadequacy and dysfunction, insecurity over my manhood. Certainly that was at work. I am not saying that others shared the same imagination with me, nor that these personal reasons activating support for the idea of revolution were generally true for males in the New Left. All I know is that it was true for me.

And yet I was convinced that violence, *all* violence, was both sexual and political in basis, and that its explanation lay in the sexual scarring of the young, particularly the sexual disfigurement of young males. It was difficult to posit manhood in America, for the values that corporate capitalism intruded into the culture and the social institutions it created were antihuman and antisexual. They were perverse.

Even then I understood rape and acts of violence by young males against women to be political acts in the specific sense that they were long-delayed reactions against authority presented to males in boyhood in the person of a dominant woman, the matriarch and the teacher. To take an extreme case, if one is a ghetto black, a young male, and fails at school under the authority of women teachers and fails at home before a strong mother, without a father, and comes of age in a deprived community where the black male is chronically unemployed or does the shit work or has to abandon his family because of welfare regulations, then one grows up feeling powerless and emasculated. In that situation one could argue that rape or other violence against women is both a sexual and a political act, a gesture indicating a desperate and short-circuited quest for manhood and moral authority as surely as does total-loss addiction and suicide by young males. Most crimes of violence are committed by young black males, sixteen to twenty-one, against women. To take it closer to the New Left, most members of the Weatherman came from middle-class, often Jewish, homes where the mother was dominant.

There was sexual politics at work on the left; a few months after the SDS convention in Chicago the Weatherman suddenly appeared during the October "Days of Rage" and tore through the streets in leathers and helmets and bikers' boots and chains, the men and women in separate cadres. And their dress and aggressive manner spoke to feelings of sexual inadequacy and powerlessness. Violence, the Weatherman thought, granted one moral authority insofar as it testified to one's courage. Perhaps that was true, although I think it testified more to estrangement and impotence. Even in 1968, when I was part of the Mathematics (Red) Commune at Columbia University during the students' protests there, I sensed something of the sexual need of young males, of myself, to be acknowledged by more powerful, older males, by institutions and personalities who had disregarded us, rendered us ineffective. And like most of the temporary, ad hoc institutions of the New Left (until the rise of the women's movement created not female dominance of the left but rather sexual separatism within it) the Columbia communes were largely male endeavors, male-dominated, where young men experienced mastery and command.

Well, that was part of the appeal of the idea of revolution

to me in 1969. In the idea were fraternity and youth and a special kind of sexual transcendence found in the employment of violence. Politics gave to violence a moral rationale. And if you were a humanist as I was—I do not mean this cynically—you required moral reasons in order to act. And one had to continue to act aggressively if one did not want to end up like the old Communist party wheel horses, like Gus Hall, like the veterans of Spain.

In the car driving to Chicago I was very conscious of the sexual nature of my participation in the left. Somewhere, perhaps in the late fifties, or maybe, as Paul Goodman noted, because my generation is the first to grow up with the certainty of the Bomb and thus to have imprinted on our minds the possibility of the end of all life, somewhere deep in my psyche was rooted a conviction of ineffectiveness before history and my rage over that fact. Manhood implied power and manly competence. It also meant establishing an equality and justice for oneself and others in society. It concerned courage before an enemy and the willingness to take ultimate risks—that is, to contend to the point of death. And the reason my romanticism entered and the idea of revolution (or "revolutionaries," for I could not think of it in any but concrete and collective terms) became warped in my mind—away from purely political-social considerations to aesthetic and sexual ones—was that I grew up believing in an ideal community of friends. In gangs. In collective male action. In the family of victims. Early in my adolescence I knew male friends who died young and a teacher who was a suicide by hanging. So I was impressed by the fragility and the shortness and the contingency of life. The romanticism existed in my response to that impression: I believed that young men who stood against the established order (i.e., against injustice), outlaws, revolutionaries, whatever, were heroic. To chance ultimate risk when you are young and strong, to chance the waste of life for an ideal or to satisfy a need central to your manhood, to your integrity, that was beautiful. Manhood was earned in the risk. And that was how I saw the dynamic of the New Left. That is what I thought revolution was partly about.

We arrived at the Chicago Coliseum on Tuesday afternoon. As we entered police and federal agents snapped our pictures. We had to wait in the vestibule of the Coliseum for the issuance of credentials. Each day the wait grew longer as the convention became more paranoid, the security check more elaborate.

Twenty minutes into the convention I got into an argument with several women and some homosexual activists over their separate rights. My response to their demands— the abolition of marriage, the removal of gender from the language, sex change on demand—was astonishment. It was here that I first encountered militant feminism. Women's liberation came at one suddenly, like a Mack truck tearing into your lane, totally unexpected, and quickly one discovered that in the most routine flirtations and in a glance held too long, danger lurked. The women were demanding a new and dramatic shift in traditional relationships, both political and carnal, and they insisted that a new seriousness be directed not only to their politics but to some remote area of their consciousness which lay outside the political and, I have to admit, outside my comprehension. There had been a shift in the structure of their being, the way in which they appreciated themselves, and this altered dramatically, at times absurdly, their mode of being in the world and thus my male response to them. For the first time women seemed confusing and threatening to me. I did not know how to respond.

On Wednesday the convention floor was crowded and I went into the balcony and sat with two friends: George, from Wisconsin, a former ADA member and now a draft-resister on his way to jail; and Jann Eller, a young laborer from Pennsylvania. We sat together and watched the convention, Jann leaning forward intently, honestly trying to learn something of value to bring back to his union. I watched him carefully. He was handsome, and he was given to smiling easily and to gentleness and he had a soft voice and a quiet modest demeanor that conflicted with the hard edge of his political statements. He interested me for many reasons, none of them sexual. The most important was the ambivalence toward violence I sensed in him, the incongruity between his physical beauty and gentleness and the conviction I had that he would end violently. It was odd. To be with him was like being with someone you would learn in a short time had fallen. I do not know if that conviction about Jann will be true in fact; I certainly responded to him in that way and that is how he survives in my memory.

We sat together in the balcony sipping Coke and watching the action on the floor below. The Progressive Labor people were easy to spot, dressed uniformly in clean work shirts and trousers or inexpensive suits and ties, with short hair, clean-shaven, looking very serious, glum, overly proletarian. They appeared to be the oldest element at the convention, certainly the most tightly organized and disciplined. They had *planned* for this convention months in advance, had packed the hall with what was a numerical majority of their entire national membership.

The non-PL delegates (I among them) were a mixture of types: hippies, crazies, a large contingent of youthful sloppy dressers, former flower children with a touch of individual style to their bellbottoms and long hair and floppy hats and wild sunglasses.

The National Office of SDS (Mike Klonsky, Bernadine Dohrn, Mark Rudd, John Jacobs, and company) was outmatched by Progressive Labor in organization, outwitted in tactics, outgunned in politics. The National Office (with whom Eric Mann and Jann Eller and I identified) had not tried to pack the convention, or if they had tried they had failed. The reason was that very few people in local SDS chapters cared to take the National Office or the national conventions seriously. Partly because of a healthy wariness of the creation of an institutional bureaucracy in SDS (that resistance to bureaucratic centralism was one of the strengths and weaknesses of the New Left) and also because the National Office traditionally had not given much direction to the local chapters, SDS was a loose kind of federation, an almost casual umbrella organization, and as a result of this casual (dis)organizational nature, it was vulnerable to seizure by any tightly disciplined, organized party functioning within it. Progressive Labor was such a party.

SDS encompassed around seventy thousand young activists. The National Office represented the majority of that seventy thousand, and that majority was not in control of the convention. Because of that, Progressive Labor used Tim McCarthy, the pro-National Office chairman, as a doormat, and piled over national secretary Klonsky, and tromped right through interorganizational secretary Bernadine Dohrn.

Wednesday, on the first important vote (over the admission of the press), the National Office lost the ballgame. Overwhelmingly. We knew who the new owners of the team were: Progressive Labor. The rest of us lost, and that was rather disorienting. The convention, by that vote, appeared to have fallen under the control of an organization that was a front for an outside party. And there we were, people who had identified with SDS for at least five years, some since its founding in 1962, and it no longer belonged to us. We never recovered from that loss.

That night Jann Eller and George and I and several others sat in our underwear in my room at the YMCA, sweating in the heat, trying to figure out what the different ideological positions of the two central factions of the convention were. I am going to briefly discuss those positions, since they more or less define the ideological split in the American left between the "democratic left" and the Trotskyists. This division, more than anything else, accounted for the decline of the New Left. And that decline is one of the concerns of this book.

At the convention *everyone* claimed to be revolutionary,

Maoist, Marxist-Leninist, socialist, anti-imperialist, antiracist, anticapitalist, communist (small C). We clung so enthusiastically to these labels because, in part, they were new to us—that is, their application by us to our lives was new. And they vibrated with echoes of history in Moscow and Petrograd and Paris and Madrid. To employ them was to declare that you were no longer a student radical playing political fun and games between the Frisbee tournaments. You were adult. Grown up. You could not be disregarded anymore. You had come of age and contended for power.

Where Progressive Labor disagreed with the non-PL delegates was on what positions were mandated by Marxism on specific contemporary issues. Here, like the popes of Rome and Avignon, the two groups were miles apart in their exegeses of the Word.

On national self-determination for Blacks, Spanish-Americans, other colonies within the Mother Country (i.e., the United States), the National Office supported the right of all exploited minorities to self-determination within and even political secession from the Mother Country. The National Office saw self-determination as a transitional state to socialism. The problems of the blacks in particular were of a special nature because of the character of white supremacy and racism in the United States. The blacks had the right to establish a revolutionary nationalism (as distinguished from "cultural" nationalism), to consolidate independent strength apart from their role as workers within the socialist revolution. In other words, they were victims twice, as blacks and as workers.

PL rejected the special nature of the blacks, refused to treat racism as anything other than a product of capitalism which would only be destroyed when capitalism itself was. The Black Panthers' demand for self-determination was attacked as petty-bourgeois nationalism, cultural chauvinism, and objectively contrary to the revolution. Thus, PL deemphasized the identity of the blacks as other than workers, because the admission of special pleading divided the proletariat.

On international liberation movements, the National Office supported the Cuban, Albanian, Chinese, and Vietnamese liberation struggles. At issue most directly was the National Liberation Front of South Vietnam and the Government of North Vietnam, both of which the National Office strongly supported.

However, PL only supported the Chinese Revolution, seeing it alone as authentically internationalist revolutionary (denying the nationalist character of much of the Chinese Communist experience). Everyone else they refused to support. North Vietnam they rejected as a sellout for negotiating with the Americans in Paris. The NLF was condemned as a counterrevolutionary force in that it allowed non-Communist elements, such as the Buddhists, into the Front. Because of these very positions on the question of international liberation movements, the National Office dismissed PL as being counterrevolutionary—i.e., it refused to support *current* revolutionary struggles around the world.

On women's liberation, the National Office supported the fight against male chauvinism. PL opposed that fight on much the same grounds as those on which they opposed the Black Panthers. That is, PL saw women's liberation as a diversionary issue in that it established women as something other than workers, giving to women, as to blacks, a noneconomic (they would say, "non-Marxist") identity. PL took a rigidly Marxist economic tack on every question, while the National Office was willing to admit that psychological, cultural, and social considerations, in addition to economic, obtained in the determination of revolutionary action.

On worker-student alliance, PL believed that students should become industrial workers full time. Period.

The National Office, on the other hand, supported a worker-student alliance (the summer work-in, where students took summer jobs in industrial plants and tried to organize the workers, was part of this concept). PL dismissed the whole idea as tokenism. National Office also sought to create a revolutionary youth movement uniting all exploited classes with the proletariat: the youth, the blacks, and other minority nations, all the victims in and of America in one alliance dedicated to the overthrow of American capitalism.

Okay. That is how we thought then, regardless of how doctrinaire it may now appear. We were attempting to make an ideology in order to act. Even I devoted myself to comprehending the contending positions. It was important to me.

On Thursday night the crack-up began.

The convention heard a passionate plea from a member of the Chicago Young Lords on the right of minority nations to self-determination. In the course of his speech he indirectly attacked Progressive Labor. He was shouted down.

The crunch came when a member of the Illinois Black Panthers came to the podium and went into a heated denunciation of Progressive Labor as a counterrevolutionary force. He called for their purge from SDS. He pleaded for the continuance of white radical support and for, again, the right of his people to self-determination. As he spoke, the Progressive Labor faction yelled, "Bullshit!" and "Petty bourgeois dog!"

Halfway into his speech, he made a fatal blunder by bringing up the subject of "pussy power," a term Eldridge Cleaver once attempted to popularize in his speeches on campuses. The PL hecklers were joined by the women's liberationists in shouting down the black male.

He blundered because he did not see male chauvinism as we saw it from our white, decidedly middle-class positions. The women among us (most of whom were from comfortable backgrounds where boredom, as Mailer noted, is a significant question) in their egocentricity elevated the inequality of the sexes to a burning issue, and they could with straight faces and obvious sincerity compare the irritants of women's oppression at the hands of white males to that of blacks suffering racism or the Vietnamese enduring imperialism. It seemed to me that this showed an insensitivity, a sexual arrogance verging on the immoral.

The Black Panther shouted out his speech, perspiring before us, going on maniacally because he was in bondage and seeking freedom from a matriarchal culture which demeaned him as a man and which Eldridge Cleaver once described and condemned in *Soul On Ice*. He understood the question of male chauvinism as a man would who was desperately compensating for the humiliation of manhood in a slave culture. He misunderstood the tenor of this largely white, young, middle-class convention. I think he believed the shouting was not over the content of his message ("pussy power") but over his use of obscenities. He charged us with being puritanical.

I watched as the convention dissolved into one hysterical shout against his words, his maleness, watched people break into acrimonious delirium, screaming obscenities, jumping up and down like demented children waving their little red books. He was a black male, speaking by default for the Panthers because all of his leaders had been jailed by the police, speaking to us, exhorting us not to abandon the black-liberation struggle, celebrating the solidarity of the left since he knew in his loins that without the active support of *white* middle-class kids, he and his fellow blacks were condemned to racial murder, that without us the police could wipe them out in obscurity with not a single liberal voice raised in protest. But if we stood with them, and if the police moved against them and in the killing slew some whites, or if Tom Hayden, God help him, was murdered in a police assault on his black brothers, then the white, liberal establishment would raise almighty hell. He knew liberals. He knew us. He knew death when he saw it loosed by indifference. He knew America and its racism and how it valued white skins, and he knew that without the shielding flesh of white kids the blacks were isolated and near defenseless, the Panthers sitting ducks. And that was precisely why he declared Progressive Labor counterrevolutionary, as more dangerous than the police. If Progressive Labor came into control of SDS, the only effective national organization on the student left, it would withdraw white radical support from the Panthers in the name of Marxism, since Progressive Labor saw the blacks as workers and nothing more.

And I thought, watching the turmoil on the floor and listening to that black voice shouting for his life, *his* life, I thought, have we all gone mad, at each other's throats like crazed fools? Don't we know that there is nobody beyond this hall who will side with us? Don't we realize at last, God damn it, after all the woeful jailings and murders borne by the movement, don't we realize that we are alone in America without each other, that it is insanity to indulge in the luxury of disunity and recrimination when all of us, to greater or lesser degree, stand in jeopardy, and all of us, the best first, the rest later, are going to have to pay blood dues to the Man?

On Friday the split in SDS was actualized. A Black Panther read a statement condemning Progressive Labor and suggesting that it be expelled from SDS. Pandemonium. More chanting, screaming, vituperation, personal attack.

Bernadine Dohrn appeared at the podium and in the confusion shouted, "All those who agree with the principle of self-determination go into the next room." She and Klonsky and Mark Rudd and those of us aligned with the National Office (about seven hundred delegates) walked into the amphitheater next door. The split had occurred. And I, like everyone else who witnessed it, regretted it. Jann turned to me and said, "It's like watching your family die. It was like the only thing I was ever proud of just shit itself to pieces. God, it makes you so damn sick, so damn mad." Sentimental, but that was how we felt.

Friday night until Saturday night the non-PL people met in the amphitheater, caucusing behind the bleachers, at night in rooms and houses trying to decide what to do. As time passed we really began to believe that Progressive Labor *was* counterrevolutionary by virtue of its position on the NLF and the Panthers and student activism. (For example, Progressive Labor opposed the Berkeley People's Park action as "bourgeois reformist.") We understood that it was impossible in the last analysis to build any kind of viable revolutionary movement with PL looming inside it. They in point of fact were not part of us.

On Saturday night we voted to move back into the convention hall. We voted to read Progressive Labor out of SDS.

We went in. The hall was quiet. Dohrn and Rudd and Klonsky and some of their supporters, under a prior agreement with PL, took the platform while the rest of us, nearly a thousand now, stood silently around the hall with the PL faction seated in the center. Dohrn read our resolution removing Progressive Labor from the organization. We left the hall to PL shouts of "Shame! Shame! Betrayal!" and we shouted in return, our fists raised to the sky, "Power to the people!"

On Sunday the SDS National Office left the Coliseum to the rump PL faction and reconstituted itself in the First Congregational Church. Mark Rudd was elected national secretary, and resolutions were approved. Already it was too late. SDS was dead as a national movement. What remained to carry its name was another front of the Progressive Labor party. The historic SDS ceased to exist. What was born in its place, what came out of what remained of the National Office collective, was the Weatherman.

I took a bus back to New York, going part way with Jann Eller. We were dead tired. And sad. And more than a little disillusioned by what had happened.

"I organize every day," Jann said, "talk to the men about

socialism, speak against the war, against racism, speak against white privilege in the union . . . and, man, I've been beat up on the job, you know, and I'm a union man . . ." He looked over at me. "So what do I tell them? SDS, where's it going? Where's the movement now? What about *us* with their goddamn political fights? There's a fucking war going on, and people die, man, and . . . hell, some of us face the shit most all the time."

From Chicago to New York I thought about Eric Mann and the others I knew at that convention, and about how much they had paid and will have to pay before they make their revolution. They had more bravery than me, more courage even in their squabbles. I thought them beautiful and I loved them, and I loved Jann with his union and his tender strength, and George with his courage facing the federal can. And I thought, it isn't right to expel Progressive Labor from SDS. The movement has to stay wide and open and loose or it will go down in defeat.

I read in the Chicago *Sun-Times* an article about how SDS was done, finished for good. And I thought, Bullshit! But I tell you even then, what with the police and the scabs and the running dogs and the dreamers and the simple-minded left-liberals distorting the movement on one side, and me and my friends, like we were sometimes drunk and silly and violent to be violent, going at each other, I thought maybe we were losers without discipline in the end, maybe we were fools fitted for death.

In the summer of 1970 I went to Boston to visit Eric Mann at the prison at Deer Island where he was serving a two-year sentence for his role in a Weatherman-organized antiwar protest at the Harvard School of International Affairs. It was a hot day. I took a taxi from the airport through the city to the slip of land edging the bay on which the prison was situated. It was an old facility, a cluster of red Victorian buildings, their gothic windows heavily barred and gray with soot, the scene Dickensian . . . the castlelike buildings built on a small rise of land by the water, charming among the trees off the stony beach; charming if one forgot the young lives imprisoned within, the Irish from South Boston, the blacks from Roxbury, the poor and under-educated.

I stood for over an hour in the heat on the gravel driveway before the prison gates, waiting for the guards to let me through to walk the several hundred yards to the visitors' building where I would be allowed to see my friend for twenty minutes. As I waited I leaned against the chain-link fence and watched in the distance young prisoners playing touch football, some of them lounging and smoking cigarettes on the stoops of the buildings under the trees bordering the playing fields. In the late fifties I once sat under similar trees at my military prep school and watched the teams clash: youths running in the heat, out of breath, their shirts off, small ID medallions hanging from chains around their necks catching the sunlight and flashing as they ran, their bodies glistening as if oiled, their sounds and cries high and indistinct across the yard. They reminded me of the boys of Chelsea in New York, Puerto Rican and Irish delinquents with whom I worked when I first came to New York from the Middle West nearly a decade before and whom I used to watch in the afternoons in the summer playing Johnny-on-a-pony and other games on Twentieth Street below my window, and whom I heard at night jiving on the stoops and (why not?) shooting up in the doorways of PS 11, their conversation indistinct, lost in the Spanish music coming from the tenements nearby.

At the prison, watching the games, I wondered what luck or cowardice or benign-indifferent Intelligence had kept me more or less free (the longest I had been in jail was six days) during the decade of the sixties when the division between political acts and criminal ones had grown vague, like the players' cries, indistinct; when what I had grown up taking for granted, certain constitutionally protected rights, was no longer part of the given. I must say that I felt guilty (perhaps that isn't the word—*disquieted*) by my freedom, as if it connoted some lack in myself, some moral inadequacy, which permitted me to remain free and unmaimed after five years or so of more than occasional activism on the left while so many others I had known were in prison or exile or otherwise run through by the years.

Watching the prisoners taking their exercise I could no longer in good conscience make a distinction between political dissent and rebellion and the crimes of the young. It was a year since the SDS convention, a year that had witnessed the Weatherman "Days of Rage" and the bombings and the birth of widespread terrorism (over four thousand bombings in the United States in that period) and yet it seemed to me that all antisocial acts—robbery, rape, even murder without passion or cause—the active criminal posture of the young itself was, in many ways, most profoundly political. I knew I had more in common with the thief than with the policeman. Not because I was a radical or because I had spent the time since the early sixties actively on the left. No, it was because I was a romantic, and as such I found violence, dissent, defiance, sedition, rebellion by the young against the old, against the past, true and (yes, declare it), beautiful.

Summer of 1970, and so many friends had fallen. People I loved and worried about and could do little to help. I lacked their courage. I used to think, well, these youths are my brothers, my comrades. (*Youths*, for by now most of the radicals I knew were five years or so younger than I.) But what drew me to them, what excited my concern for them, what love there was, was something more deeply, peculiarly American than Marxist notions of solidarity and socialist brotherhood. No, it was something about the adoptive son in America, the street kid up against it, the working-class boy who in similar ways also obsessed (that is the word) Whitman and Hart Crane and Paul Goodman, although unlike me they refrained from giving a political content to that obsession. Maybe all those years, even now, it was sons I was scouting for, seeking to protect.

Now, after the summer of 1970, what I want to tell you about is my friendship with some of these young men, and also something about what took the place of activism when it began to fade from my life, and finally to tell you about my relationship with some older, more celebrated people— Mailer, Greer, Warhol, Williams, and others—not because they are representative of the movement—certainly they are apart from my generation—but because these people, whether by chance or design I am not sure, were involved with me, some more intimately than others. At the beginning of the seventies they made or reinforced their tenuous relations with the movement through an event I organized and through my life, when we all found ourselves skirting on the movement's edges, never dipping in.

So, to deal with what happened to us on the left I can only tell you what happened to me. And to do that I have to tell you something of my relationship with these public men and women after the collapse of SDS. In so doing I make no claim to speak for the movement. I speak for myself. Yet I am immodest enough to believe that my reactions to the period in history, the close of it anyway, which I lived through, are representative of many others who, like me, came to a position of defiance and dissent within America in the early sixties and are now at a loss for what to do.

I know what brought me to the left and holds me now: it is what I sensed that afternoon watching the prisoners play, those young men on the other side. You see, they continue to speak to me of courage and of want, of history coming like a thief in the night to take its due, of the crimes of a race catching up with it through the unhappiness and rage of its sons, of what Norman Mailer once referred to as the armies of the final Armageddon forming in the seeds of men not yet born. I could sense it forming there, in the bodies and minds of those young men in the Boston prison yard who had been labeled for life as outlaw. And to the degree that I was outside the prison fence and thus within the law, to that degree I stood as enemy or at least as privileged outsider in the fierce world those young men defined in their play in that prison compound. How I envied them!

part one

BYE, BYE
MISS
AMERICAN
PIE

1

A year later. May 1971. I had dinner with Dave McReynolds, a leading functionary of the pacifist War Resisters League. McReynolds told me of the precarious financial shape the Peoples Coalition for Peace and Justice (PCPJ) was in as a result of the May Day demonstrations in Washington weeks before. The Peoples Coalition was the largest and most effective antiwar organization still functioning in the United States, and its financial health had a direct bearing on the health of the entire peace movement. Fear, indifference over the war, Vietnamization, ideological splits in the movement, the collapse of SDS, the increasing demand of legal defense on movement finances and manpower all contributed to the financial bankruptcy of the Peoples Coalition. And if you opposed the war, then the economic stability of the Coalition was a matter of pressing concern: if the Coalition went under, much of the organized peace movement might sink with it.

After dinner I went uptown to the Park Avenue apartment of Senator and Mrs. Jacob Javits. I had known Mrs. Javits for some time, considered her a friend, and while politically we had little in common, I found her fascinating as a person, rather electric and dangerous in the way beautiful women married to powerful men often are: the caged spirit, the sense of mischief and panic. She lived in a world without consequences for her, and therefore in one without much meaning.

with mailer at the senator's

Mrs. Javits called me, inviting me for drinks, telling me that Norman Mailer would be there; and that was catnip to me, since I considered him the best writer alive, the one you had to contend with, for he was, as he boasted, the Champ (even here he has me defining him in his own terms). In a way not clear to me he was a father figure (I think he would dislike anyone saying that) and a sexual competitor. No, that is not right, not a competitor, but an explorer or hunter tracking wherever he smelled power, the sexual the most potent scent among them, a man whose instincts were dangerously sound and, in a strange manner, presciently revealing. The truth I read in him always came to me through the ear, through the noise of urgency and passion . . . well, Mailer, through his life and work, told me secrets about myself I did not want to know, which I resisted, yet which I needed to know; for like a father giving you the grim truth about the green queens and bleeding dirt, Mailer belted you until he got your attention and then, without the weakness of sentiment, laid it on you even if it meant total loss. I identified with Mailer in this way: as a powerful man *in* the way. He was someone I wanted to take a shiv to, and then knew the courage would always fail me at the chance—simply to know the remorse and, hell, the rep of having laid him low. There was no way, none, except with a steel blade, to bring him down.

Spiritually Mailer's relationship to the movement was the same as my own, his attention caught by unreason and violence hulking through the streets, through history, in a manner driven by the most intimate of masculine insecurities. I often thought that we were both on some kind of butch (death) trip without a meal ticket in the end, but the act was dated and nobody was buying the rough-trade tough-guy number anymore, most especially not the women. So we felt put upon. While Mailer was not really a left activist, when he did choose to appear at demonstrations he carried himself like a street angelic, a tough after trouble, slugging marshals, careening over police lines. Not an activist, he maintained a proprietary, avuncular quarrel with the New Left, and his instinct again was so acute that he usually knew what the left was up to—although his evidence came at a safe distance—and he had the balls to declare it, which was one of the reasons he was roundly hated by many young radicals. He had a big mouth when it came to the emperor's clothes. So it was his readiness to give unasked-for advice to the young, plus his life style (some thought him a "culture vulture," an opportunist ripping off the movement for the benefit of the press), which placed him at best in an ambiguous position vis-à-vis the New Left.

At the Javitses' I started to speak to Mailer about the money problems of the Peoples Coalition, but his mind was on other things. He wanted to know about the May Day demonstrations, about the massive disruption of Washington traffic, the street trashing, the thirteen thousand arrests. He was concerned about the future of the New Left and so was I, but perhaps both of us should have been more concerned with what we were doing there in the Senator's apartment.

Also there were Germaine Greer, the feminist celebrity, several other writers, and a number of rich people. I believed the Senator shared complicity with Congress in the war in Indochina (which is to say, complicity in murder), not only by the fact that he voted the war appropriations; additional complicity came in his refusal to campaign actively against the war and in his political support of the Republican administration waging the war.

I was aware of the intimate relationship that had grown up between left-liberal establishment circles, the well-intentioned rich and their left-liberal political allies, and the radicals. It had reached ridiculous proportions, based as it was on a psychological symbiosis, an unacknowledged interdependency that was mutually subverting. The rich were both corrupting—because nearness to wealth desensitizes—and corruptible—because they tended to be politically unknowledgeable and morally vacant.

The left-liberal rich were bored with traditional liberal democracy, sharing with the radicals a contempt for the official parties, for politicians in general, and for the corporate state that produced and protected their privilege. And, worse, they were haunted by the sense that history was ignoring them (their *kids* were ignoring them!), that they had lost touch and could no longer affect history as it was affecting them. They felt disregarded and impotent, a feeling, as I noted earlier, that I shared. In short, they believed that the connection between themselves and the energy centers in the nation, between themselves and the new sources of change, which they saw in terms of radical and alternative culture youth, had broken. They longed to reestablish the link. Patrician left-liberals sensed that something was at work in the country which they neither understood nor felt comfortable with and therefore could not harness and manipulate . . . something, a movement, whose sexual energy and cultural creativity they envied and, feeling threatened, resented. Resented because the energy was *sexual,* whether it expressed itself in gay liberation or women's movements or the communal coupling of the young. Or in violence. Politics, first through language (the Free Speech Movement) and then through sexual liberation and finally through violence, had been sexualized, and the thrust of that sexual-political assault was aimed at the parents, the established white, heterosexual, male-dominated political arrangements. And where that attack was most subversive was in its ridicule of the nuclear family.

Additionally, much of their interest in radicals and in supporting radical causes, which they did to an astonishing degree, patently came out of a necessity to relieve guilt. I am not implying that many of the rich did not act from thoroughly honorable motives (guilt is honorable), nor that they were incapable of honest opposition to war and racism or other causes. It was simply that I suspected the depth of the sincerity of wealth when it was limited to giving a small (tax deductible, of course) proportion of the income earned from profits off the war or from the exploitation of labor. And while I agreed with Abbie Hoffman that all money was washable, and therefore was not especially concerned about the sources of the funds that came the movement's way, I was not so insensitive as to credit the rich with much charity because of their largess. As Lenin said, when the revolution hangs the ruling class it is the bourgeoisie who will sell the rope. While in the short run it was probably in the economic interest of the left-liberal rich to support the peace movement, in the long run I could not help but believe that the young people trained and educated by that movement would, some of them, turn to other matters not in their interest when the war was over. And finally, it must be remembered that for a time in New York, before the term "radical chic" was coined, it was fashionable to be mildly left. While that was not a terribly important consideration to the rich, I was positive it was one of the motives behind the relationship between the rich and those committed to ending their privilege.

To repeat, there was a strong sexual element at work. Radicals like myself, through media-created environments, were given a violent image. And since in America violence was so often associated with courage (it was in my mind) and therefore with manhood, there was a definite aura of slumming sexuality around radical males. That should not have been surprising, since the tradition of sexually slumming beneath and outside your class was strong among the leisure classes in the West, most clearly to be seen in the piss-elegant homosexual's taste for rough trade.

So much for the left-liberal rich. What about the radicals? By May 1971 some of us perceived that the movement was in decline, at least temporarily, although that was a perception whose truth I refused to admit. So much of my identity and self-respect and sexual self-image was involved in the street activities of the left that I could not, did not want to contemplate its end. What would I become then, without the movement? An old irrelevancy like Gus Hall and his

Communist party? The dread of that future (I was nearly thirty years old) was beginning to leak into my life.

Nevertheless, the decline of the movement could be judged on one hand by its diminished financial prospects (and thus, correspondingly, the increased if demeaning importance of the rich to us) and by our notable inability to organize masses of antiwar demonstrators. The days of half millions before the Lincoln Memorial were over. Even then, if I had had the courage to look, I could have seen within myself the beginnings of disillusionment with activism, with its effectiveness and its appropriateness to the times and to my own life. After so many years one begins to wonder whether there are not more efficient ways to grip the levers of power than by sitting down in Pentagon corridors or trashing the Riggs Bank. That I would think in terms of "efficiency" showed a certain caution come from age.

However, radicals *as* radicals continued to meet the rich. We needed them. We needed their money and their encouragement and the necessary confirmation of our importance which their attentions provided. I know myself that it was tremendously ego-boosting to be paid attention to by famous and powerful men. And that was understandable, remembering that I was drawn to activism in part because of a sense of being disregarded by powerful men who controlled the institutions that directly affected the lives of my friends and myself.

The year before, for example, Senator and Mrs. Javits had invited a few demonstrators to their apartment in Washington after our attack on the Justice Department and march on the White House protesting the Cambodian invasion. That is, some of us went to the Javitses' Watergate apartment around midnight, our clothes smelling of smoke and tear gas, where we had drinks with the Senator and his wife after, only hours before, attempting to make insurrection against the government he represented. I do not know on which side the corruption (or confusion) was greater.

This I know: coming into the apartment in my muddy

boots and leather jacket, wearing a cowboy hat, I felt tough and sexually aggressive as a result of the long hours of running in the streets, and my sexual high was burnished by the slightly contemptuous attitude I felt toward my host, the Senator, for welcoming us there. And yet I felt no *self*-contempt for being there. The situation was difficult for all parties. Not that real political embarrassment was at its source; it was difficult because of the sexual tension in the room. I and my friend keyed up, stoned on possibilities, ready for rape or rumble. Nothing happened.

When we left my friend asked me, "Why did we go there?"

"I like them," I said. Too easy an answer. My feelings were more ambivalent than that. I do not know if it was a writer's vice or a matter of weak principles or perversity. I was fascinated to see what the Senator was like hours after bloodshed and jailings and gas in his capital city. And this: I wanted to show off, to brandish it, to strut.

My friend replied, "They're my enemies." He may have been right. He is now in federal prison for antiwar activities. *They are my enemies.* I had been wrong to go.

All this I remembered in talking to Mailer a year later in New York, again at the Javitses'.

Norman Mailer said, "You [the New Left] have no program. You guys don't understand history. You make a mistake there. You ain't going nowhere."

I disagreed about the lack of a program, although I was never very big on programs. SDS's original Port Huron statement stood, and to me, at least, it remained an adequate if increasingly moderate program. It espoused reformist measures leading to democratic socialism in the United States, and it advocated confrontation politics and participatory democracy. But I had to admit to Mailer that, yes, it appeared that the antiwar movement was not going much of anywhere. Here was the contradiction: if socialism meant anything to me morally, it meant a profound respect for the human person—and that was why I had difficulty philosophically accepting the left's drift toward reactive violence, even though I reasoned it was the only way to actually radicalize a system as deeply entrenched as American capitalism. And psychological currents within me tugged me toward violence; there was a need in me to be near it which was both frightening and satisfying. Like so many others, I was caught up in a contradiction that was frustrating and bewildering, doubly so for me since, as I have stated, there were strong sexual and cultural reasons that made the employment of violence attractive to me. I was unable to conceive of revolution or manhood without the acceptance of its possibility, maybe even its inevitability.

So Mailer and I argued about history and about the political uses of violence.

I told Mailer that several weeks before in Central Park, I had seen a boy about nine years old sitting on a bicycle with the handlebars pushed forward and the seat low, carrying a phony gas tank like a motorcycle's in front—Captain America at age nine, helmeted, with leather jacket and boots, and lighting up a joint. "We've gotten to your kids, Norman. At nine, and he's me at twenty-nine." Or I, on New Year's Eve, with a Weatherman friend of mine, a friend I have dug since we sat in the West End bar across from Columbia University years ago and talked about scoring, both of us drunk and raging through the Village early in the morning, bitterly cold, hurling chunks of ice through store windows and smashing the windshields of expensive cars with a crutch we had lifted at a party. And I considered myself a rational man. But I was a joy-boy and violence was the john.

Violence on the left; it had come to that, and the explanation was wound up in the sexual scarring of the young. Several weeks before, I told Mailer, I had had drinks with the Weatherman friend. I had not seen him since December, and I thought I had lost·him for good when the Weatherman collectives broke up into small affinity groups and went underground. He called me one day and we got together and I realized, after talking with him, that his basic character had not changed much since the Columbia disorders in 1968, which was the turning point in many of our lives.

His primary motivation was the same: his essential decency and the gentleness of his spirit were apparent as I listened to him talk with an icy detachment tinged by trained suspicion (he protected his associates by always being cautious in what he said). He was still my friend. It strikes me now that we were both romantically aware of how unusual our meeting was, that he was numbered by the police and in a sense already part of history and was living his life in light of his death. I trusted him. My regard for him, after learning of the hell he had been through, the agony of spirit, to reach his commitment, my regard for him increased, for an intolerable grief motivated him, an anguish. I had known him so long, and the content of our friendship had been so overwhelmingly apolitical, that it was hard to grasp him limited to this role. (One note: the night of the blackout in New York we were together and we went into Broadway and mingled with the crowd and drank and watched a lame panty raid on a Barnard College dormitory fizzle out. He was full of laughter. We played. Years ago.) And to see him much later, as I told Mailer, when there existed a point beyond which I could not go, when this Weatherman, my friend, and I had reached the outer limits—my response to that fact was to envy his courage and to feel guilty because I was incapable of joining him underground. I hadn't the grit for it. He was like a young warrior-priest who had taken vows and was under discipline and who now consciously steeled himself against the past. He had lost his sense of play.

"What does he want?" Mailer asked. "What is he after?"

"To bring the war home. To make New York Saigon." True. He was caught in a contradiction with me in that he went beyond logic to assert a very desperate and profoundly human hope: by the selective use of violence, violence itself could be defeated. Sometimes, it was said, men must kill the killers to stop the murder. So my friend wanted to bring the war home and to spread violence like jissom over the body of

America, paste it across the American consciousness until America, like Vietnam, suffocated on death. His mistake was to assume that death was foreign to man, that violence repelled him (how wrong he was!), because man, like Ionesco's Bérenger, longed to be cured of death. Finally, he believed in the essential goodness and decency of the average man. That was his populism and his democratic myth. His belief that the average citizen would rebel when the State went totalitarian was the faith behind the terrorist and the bomber, that violence, like a knife through cloth, sundered liberal corporate democracy and made way for the fascism that prepared the people for revolution. Pipe dreams.

I told Mailer that my Weatherman friend was twenty-eight. "I'm getting old too," I said. Mailer laughed.

"There's already a break between the two generations in the New Left. Those of us who found our politics in the early sixties and the high-school kids coming into the streets now. We don't even communicate anymore. We don't see violence in the same terms."

Mailer said he appreciated the appeal of violence. And I said, without irony, "Yes, it's a way to create your manhood."

He nodded. "You're crazy, man. If you ever win that'll be why. Because you're nuts!" He punched me lightly on the arm, laughing.

Later I sat in the study with Mrs. Javits listening to Ray Charles's "Crying Time" on the phonograph. I sat close to her, my arm around her, conscious that Mailer was somewhere snorting around the apartment with Germaine Greer on his tail. The sexual tensions were heavy in the place. It was late, and we were all into the booze, and a kind of mellowness was in the room. Mailer came up behind me and put his arms around me in a hammerlock. I got up from the couch and went into what I thought was a boxer's stance and slugged him on the arm. We play-boxed a minute, awkwardly, Mailer with his fists up and grinning.

I bring this up because the fall into a boxer's stance was

false for me (I was no boxer) and I had slipped into the role
assigned to me by Mailer, who knew me not through friendship initially but through reading my first book about the
left, which was riddled with its (my) violence. I think he
saw me as tougher than I was, and I, knowing his reputation,
tried to complement him by being as scruffy and rugged as
credibility would permit. I felt as if we were two bullies meeting on neutral turf between rumbles, on a school play-
ground, and grinning at the mutual handsome class we
possessed.

My language became fouler than usual for me; I had the
urge to call Mrs. Javits, a very proper lady, a fucking chick
and to talk about the number of pussy belts nailed to the
wall, as if Mailer and I were tackles compensating for losing
a game by boasting of our sexual prowess, the claims made
not in our speech but in our manner. And in looking back
that seems rather adolescent, even distasteful to me, not because I would see Mailer that way (God knows there is in him
the Fitzgerald fiction of the old running back obsessed by the
memory of the longest pass), but adolescent in that I could
with such ease disavow the majority of my being and choose
one specific aspect of my *fantasy* self and offer it to Mailer
as myself. Why? Because Mailer was leader of the Hell's
Angels. I was on his turf and I felt compelled to prove myself tougher (the same dynamic at work in confrontations
with the police).

Christ, the mutilations we practice on ourselves short of
violence. Maybe, in this regard, play-boxing with Mailer,
what was at work there, muted, was the kind of need for
transcendence which drove the Weatherman to enforce
homosexuality in their heterosexual communes as a device
for the making of subversives. In the United States, in a sex-
rejecting, sex-repressive culture, somehow everything seemed
to be purchased with the coin of sexual self-disfigurement.
You became a caricature of yourself—Super Butch—because, say with Mailer and what he represented as a writer

and a man, the competitiveness you felt and the distrust and wariness were so great that you sought without design to one-up him at his own game. But you had the edge of years on him, and thus, like a bird swelling its breast in courting, you verbally puffed the size of your meat—what you had as men which made you part of the gang. You played it mean. And that was a dead end. It was nowhere.

Early that morning we wound up together in a bar in Midtown.

Mailer said the New Left suffered a failure of imagination. And then he asked where I thought we, the New Lefties, would end.

"We're going to end like Gus Hall."

Mailer, into the booze like me, shook his head. He was sitting back in the seat with his hands in his jacket pockets, his shoulders hunched, and it was that gesture, the pocketed hands, which reminded me of Gus Hall.

"Gus what?"

"Gus Hall. Head of the Communist party."

"Oh." Mailer unimpressed.

"He's got the largest collection of Socialist Realist art in the Western Hemisphere."

"Really?" Mailer was beginning to go dim.

"And he lives in Yonkers in a two-story house and putters in his basement with a Sears fix-it lathe. He wears Robert Hall suits. He believes an American proletariat exists."

"Believes an American . . . ?"

"And he reads *The Daily World.* Daily. He watches Monty Hall on television and discusses him seriously as an example of postindustrial capitalist decadence."

"Monty who?"

"He takes William Buckley seriously. *William Buckley!*"

Mailer shrugged. Disbelief.

"He vacations in Miami Beach, and he thinks Kosygin is

fun. Half the party's membership is government agents and he boasts about secrecy. He still thinks it's 1946. And I'm going to end up like him. A Red optimist!"

Mailer spilled his drink.

2

In 1965 I was chairman of a students' speakers' bureau at Columbia and as such I was instrumental in bringing Gus Hall to the University, where he gave one of the first speeches against the Vietnam War. It was a fine speech, and while I did not have a high regard for the Communist party, I did develop a fondness for and, more important, an intense curiosity about its leader, Gus Hall.

How could a man spend his life that way? Which is another way of asking how a man could be so happy and well adjusted (Hall was nothing if not well adjusted) who had surrendered his intellectual independence to a monolithic party.

Gus Hall, in addition to being a former steelworker and a founder of a metalworkers' union in the thirties (and sharing with me a similar background: both of us spent our boyhoods in Minnesota), was a writer and, by the loose standards of the American left, an intellectual worker. Thus, my interest in Hall was related to my interest in the left in general and in my concern with the function of the writer in the United States.

Like everyone else, I was also concerned about the general state of intellectual disrepair in the United States, and in some manner Gus Hall—as a monument to clean hopes despoiled, to a shoddiness brought on by age and defeat—was pertinent to my understanding of that disrepair and to my recent need to understand what drew me

the
mountains
of
mongolia

to political activism and how it was similar to and in what
ways different from what made me a writer. In some complex
manner the rise of the New Left, and my own participation in
it, was related to political and moral disintegration in American civilization, to a form of barbarism of the spirit which
tolerated, even encouraged, the fragmentation of the community into exurban camps, the building of highways and the
promotion of an architecture and city-suburban planning
that was, like the political-economic system financing it,
contemptuous of human scale and need. I had learned something from Paul Goodman of the role of the writer and the
complicated relationship between that function and the
political life. In the smallest way I was only beginning to
suspect that there might be a natural conflict between the
writer and the political activist, that—this was the terror—
to be one, you were obliged to betray so subtly, through a
dynamic still indistinct to me, the other. Part of the betrayal
was that it diminished your capacity to recognize your own
bad faith.

April 1971, immediately before the May Day demonstrations in Washington, I spent several hours talking with Gus
Hall at Communist party headquarters in New York. The
Communist party was one of fifty organizations on the steer-
ing committee of the Peoples Coalition for Peace and Justice. I was giving time to the Coalition as an organizer and
a fund-raiser. We discussed movement affairs, although Gus
continually turned the conversation around to the subject of
the party. I think he saw a potential convert in me.

Communist party headquarters is a four-story, red-brick
townhouse that once served as the offices of the Vanderbilt
family. Across the street, in brownstones with windows
darkened by dirt, the FBI sits behind the glass monitoring
the doorways to CP headquarters and tapping the phones, a
fact of life in which Gus Hall takes pride. The government
still *cares*.

To get to Gus Hall's hideaway office on the top floor, you climb the stairs past rooms painted institutional green, past smudged walls and naked light fixtures and yellowing wall posters of Lenin and Marx, curling at the edges like old campaign flyers, past a broken icebox abandoned on the landing, a FREE ANGELA sticker pasted to its side. In the rooms, in the tiny cubbyholes off the narrow corridors cluttered with packing crates, old men sit around tables arguing about the revisionists and the left-wing adventurists (i.e., the New Left), about the betrayals and the purges and the disputes they alone remember, unresolved after fifty years. This is the party that for ten years, ever since the New Left was born with the SDS at Port Huron, has been telling us it is the "Home of the Revolution" . . . waving the bloody flags and, before we produced our own martyrs, throwing the Abraham Lincoln Brigade in our faces the way Nixon once employed the Alger Hiss affair to intimidate Republican irregulars. Gus Hall sees the party veterans as the advance guard of the revolution, the men who will finally seize the American capitalist pie. But what I see are old men given over to the memories of failure in Detroit and Madrid, purges and death. I see defeat.

On the second floor is the trophy room, which is a repository of the battle flags of the American left, or at least that part of it influenced, to put it diplomatically, by the CP. It is an eerie thing to enter that room, eerie if while young you ever had visions of red flags flying over Washington. For in the trophy room one is impressed by a raffish, lost grandeur, a sense of opportunities blown, history muffed, by a tacky, squirrelly sadness. Posters crowded between the filthy windows condemn racism and warism and child labor and militarism and Hitlerism and the Huns, capitalism and Zionism and Huey Long. And beside the fireplace, the trophy case itself—a bronze statuette of two fierce workers gripping an unfurled flag (*This was specifically presented to Gus Hall by the Metal and Foundry Workers of the City of Omsk, Siberia*)

. . . an eight-volume history of the CP of East Germany given to Gus Hall by Comrade Walter Ulbricht . . . and over the fireplace, deer antlers festooned with dust like Australian pines hung with Spanish moss, antlers *presented to Gus Hall by the General Secretary of the Mongolian CP, Comrade Y. Tsedenbal, as a reminder of a hunting trip in the mountains of Mongolia with the leaders of the People's Republic.*

The mountains of Mongolia. It was days before I would find myself in jail with thirteen thousand other protesters in Washington, and Gus Hall is telling me about the mountains of Mongolia and how I must go there sometime and how the party is the Wave of the Future and how, sooner or later, you kids will wake up to the fact that *there is no revolution outside the party.* No cadres, no vanguard without it, no hope outside the party Gus Hall leads.

Gus Hall moves into a room like a grinding, slow, old locomotive, chunky body swaying from side to side, his shoulders, like cement slabs, thrust back (his sense of dignity is housed there), his arms hanging down, unmoving, carried along like two logs sewn into his jacket. Gus Hall is given to back-slapping and bone-breaking handshakes and bad, clean jokes and jamming his large hands into his jacket pockets à la Kennedy à la Mailer, stretching the cloth out of shape. He is a good man yet a loser, and to see him is to wheel the mind back to where he is from, to think of striking laborers sitting at dusk in saloons in company towns named Hibbing and Ely and Iron and Atkins, telling the same lousy cornball jokes Gus continues to tell, and cursing the Pinkertons and the scabs in the rough Marxist passion of the thirties.

Gus nods and grins and equivocates. "I've an optimistic outlook," he says, his speech accented by his Norwegian origins. "We're high here at the party. We're with it. Boy, up to a couple of years ago I'd've said socialism wouldn't take place in America in my lifetime. But now, *wow!*" He grins triumphantly and takes a bite from his tuna sandwich. He sips his coffee. "More and more people, *even teen-agers,* see the party as the necessary part of revolutionary development in the United States. We're closer to the *scene* now. . . ."

It occurs to me that as self-consciously as Hubert Humphrey wearing Peter Max ties and dyeing his hair patent-leather black and wearing make-up and bubbling with terms like "Groovy!" instead of "Golly!" Gus Hall has adopted the verbal badges, four years late, of the flower children. Will they ever get in step?

"We're very much hip. We're growing! Especially in the South. It's like a new day for the party. Man, you kids [I am twenty-eight] got to come aboard. We're where it's at!"

So it was the idea of ending like this man that obsessed me. An optimist by necessity, trapped in his role, too late, too late. This was it: I was frightened of losing grip on integrity, the moral courage or humor, the irony or whatever it is whose loss renders a man's soul to decay and memory and the solace of illusion and drives him into moral and intellectual exhaustion. That I never wanted to happen.

No, to be frank, sometimes I was tempted by the thought of slipping through the history of leftist struggle here, slipping through, yet retaining my radical credentials by signing on with Gus Hall and company and taking one of those wooden swivel chairs with the squeaky springs behind the plywood desks at party headquarters. It crossed my mind. Anyone who tells you that New Leftists, that radicals, were not attracted by the idea of becoming organization functionaries for thirty years and then retirement, anyone who says that is out to lunch. Because one of the things we have done since the formation of SDS is to try to create organizations with impressive names and secretariats and hierarchies in which to play out our fantasies of status and revolution with mimeograph machines rather than blood. We, who ridiculed functionaries and bureaucracies. Because what has now taken hold of many of us—I am speaking of those of us who were young in the sixties and are now pushing thirty and for the first time grappling with booze and barbiturates and sleeplessness and sexual disorder and the creeping sense of political failure, of having been in history and having fucked it—what has taken hold of us is the need—when real youth is gone and we find ourselves feeling nearly out of touch with the generation of teen-agers pressing our rear—the need to find the cubbyhole with the green metal desk, that dusty office in some leftist organization or a place on the staff of some crummy, dull, left-wing periodical, something through which we can maintain our political credentials and let the world pass. Something to relieve the goddamn guilt coming in the suspicion that neither revolution nor manhood is created anywhere but in the streets. No more to take the clubbing and the jails.

Because, you see, we find ourselves winded in the race, scared in a different way now before charging cops . . . growing sentimental, understanding Tom Hayden's desire for children, family. We find ourselves nearly thirty and beyond and having known brothers and sisters shot down, jailed, exiled, sold out, betrayed. So if you went through Berkeley and Chicago and Columbia and the Pentagon and believed, as most of us did, that revolution was around the corner, and discovered, five, ten years later, that what was around the corner was Richard Nixon, was the fifties all over again, was more tear gas and cops and bullets coming through bedroom doors at night, well, the party then, the political bureaucracies, appear attractive. Safe. Oh, to be a Dave McReynolds, a functionary with the War Resisters League, to speak at small colleges, to get to bed at night, to die in your sleep.

It was that option or what other? To take the literary route and watch your political faith decline from hope into contempt, to end like Gore Vidal with your politics fueled solely by envy, cynicism, and contempt? And if you did not become a functionary and if you did not want to watch hope and the sense of justice bled out of you, what could you do to keep your hand in? You could get arrested at decorous sit-ins. You could give money. You could adopt the Liberal

Policy: you benched yourself and cheered. *You organized benefits!*

So it was in May 1971, in Washington, demonstrating. They were a fiasco, the May actions. I sat in Dupont Circle with a demonstration of crazies and Weatherpeople and street-kid angelics zonked out on meth or dex or coke or Ritalin or God knows what shit, I squatted there with the kids screaming and running and the cops picking them off and I groped at my eyes because they were gas-sprayed and watering and my contact lenses were floating with my tears off my face. I gave up. I lay flat on the grass, To hell with it. I am too old for it. Been through it too often. Been arrested too much.

And I thought of old Gus Hall up there in Yonkers driving his Plymouth to the deli, rising in the morning to write an editorial for *The Daily World* condemning us May Day demonstrators as a pack of crazy left-wing adventurers, dope fiends, perverts, barbarians with too much physical courage and too little sense. And I thought, He's probably right! Fagged out, worn through, about to be arrested . . . what am I doing here with these zanies? Why not go the academic route and speak at union teas about democratic socialism and write unreadable books about it? Why not become a parlor liberal like Max Lerner or, God forbid, Michael Harrington? Tight-assed and making your politics in *The Militant* (groan) *The Guardian* (zzzzz) *The Progressive* (belch)? Why not? Because it does not work. I knew that as well as I knew running with stoned youngsters through Dupont Circle trashing the Riggs Bank . . . running, wheezing and coughing from the tear gas and, too, the sheer amount of nicotine and booze and what other adult American *un-*Yippie poison soiling my system . . . that also does not work.

Four days in the clink, in the central lockup, crammed with eleven other demonstrators in hundred-degree heat in a six-by-seven-foot steel cell with a broken toilet and pee on the floor and bad breath and one piece of bologna and two slices of bread and no sex and going whacko, and what was

on my mind? The war? Sex? Getting out of the can? No!
Gus Hall! I think, I'm falling to pieces. *We're going to end
like old Gus! Something must be done!*

What I did was to organize the Remember the War Benefit for the Peoples Coalition for Peace and Justice at the
Cathedral of St. John The Divine in New York in December
1971.

3

The idea for the benefit at the cathedral developed in my conversations with Dave McReynolds. It was the only means we could devise that might raise, in a short time, the money and affirmative publicity needed by the Peoples Coalition.

About three weeks after the idea was first proposed, I spoke with Dave Dellinger, who was in Colorado, and with Sid Peck, who was a professor at MIT and the chief officer of the Coalition. It was agreed that I would serve temporarily as organizer for the benefit since there was no one else available, and that within two months we would hold a meeting with Dellinger and Rennie Davis and work out the final arrangements for the affair. In order to get preliminary support for the event one of the first persons I called was Norman Mailer.

My approaching Mailer speaks not only of my admiration for him as a writer but of my conception of the Writer.

I was part of a generation of writers who were taught the ideas of existentialism and absurdism at American universities. In the process I learned a lot of nonsense because, unfortunately, serious writing had to a significant degree been taken over by academics. Many writers were supported by university appointments and grants, their literary reviews subsidized, the critical boundaries of their art determined by academic literary careerists.

For example, I was made to read and admire Heming-

aquarius
hesitates,
his hand
on her rump

way, Camus, Malraux, Sartre, and other pre- and postwar writers whose work was taught to me in the context of their lives, writers presented to me as men larger than life who lived heroically. With the possible exception of Hemingway, however, they wrote about how there were no longer any heroes. It was a baffling contradiction between biography and art. However, I think it gave me and my contemporaries a fierce dedication to the integrity of art, an undoubtedly elitist idea that art could only be created by men of active good faith.

There were many good writers in America, but there were only a few who did not in the end betray my expectations of them, who remained true to a conception of the role of the writer, a heroic and thus romantic vision that I first embraced in college. Writers were to be judged not only by what they wrote but also by how they lived, by whether their acts were consistent with the vision of their art.

To go back a moment, my own political development was from pacifism in the early sixties to a more militant social democratic position of resistance. With the birth of the Weatherman collectives in 1969, it became a voyeuristically revolutionary one, which is a clumsy way of saying that since the autumn of 1969 my distrust and disrespect for American political and corporate institutions and the commanding values behind them had developed to the point where I could justify and indeed welcome their violent overthrow. Nevertheless, I knew I had not the physical courage to engage in violent, conspiratorial, extraconstitutional activities; I had not the guts to join an affinity group and go underground. More and more, history seemed novelistic to me, I an observer and, at the same time, with my friends, a character in that novel. It took an act of will to overcome my natural passivity and to participate in demonstrations, protests, and other acts that involved violence. And yet I had mustered that will many times.

My appreciation of Mailer was that his own development was somewhat similar to my own and therefore (to the degree to which my life was representative in whatever way of others in the left) was relevant to the left. He was among a small tribe of writers who remained open to history and who constantly sided with the victim against the oppressor. In other words, he fit the notion of the writer that I had received in college, largely through the influence of Malraux and Camus.

Mailer had written in *Advertisements for Myself:* "Being a man is the continuing battle of one's life, and one loses a bit of manhood with every stale compromise to the authority of any power in which one does not believe." All of which led me to believe that both a writer's integrity and his manhood compelled him to undertake a measure of public involvement in political action against illegitimate authority. Ah, Mailer! How I loved him. Mailer in rugged engagement with the age. He possessed such little caution. His life and work courted risk beautifully, pursued it. They were enhanced by violence and, like some magnificent ocean predator caught on Hemingway steel, they were snagged to death.

Mailer was in Maine. I called him there about speaking at the benefit and joining the committee sponsoring it.

"It's a waste of time," he said.

"Norman, we're *heavily* in *debt!* The entire movement's at the cleaners'!" I was surprised by his skepticism. It sank me in panic.

"How much in debt?" Not really interested.

"About sixty thousand dollars. That's a conservative estimate."

"My God! From what?"

"From what?" I went momentarily blank. "Legal costs stemming from the May Day demonstrations. And there are several thousand draft resisters and antiwar activists still in the can." I treaded water, cursing myself for not having pressed Dellinger for more precise reasons for our monumental indebtedness. What I knew was too inexact for Mailer. "We have to get them out of jail. We're responsible for them. *We want to stop the war!*" I was reduced to bad preaching.

"What you're doing ain't worth shit. It isn't going to stop the war."

"It'll help."

"How?"

"Well . . ."

"A few *days* maybe? Maybe it'll stop the war several days earlier?"

"That might mean several hundred lives." I felt like a clothing salesman.

"I doubt it."

"We need money!"

"And I have work to finish."

"Well, think about it," I said and hung up.

I thought I had lost him. It depressed me terribly. How could he refuse? When he was asked to run for Mayor of New York he accepted even though he knew that if he won the election "he would never write again . . . but he would have his hand on the rump of History, and Norman was not without such lust." So I thought, if we only had some sort of *office* to offer Mailer, maybe then . . .

4

In July, several days before my twenty-ninth birthday, I was in Chicago with Tennessee Williams. He was there with a production of his new play, *Outcry*. I had known Williams for some time, we were close friends, and while I was not with him in Chicago in order to enlist his aid on the benefit, I did use the opportunity to speak to him about the antiwar struggle and about organizing a fundraising event for the Peoples Coalition. Williams was incensed about the war and frustrated because he knew of no way to engage himself personally and dramatically in the antiwar movement. I offered the Remember the War Benefit in December as a possible beginning point for his public engagement with the movement. Williams desired to connect with radical youth, to catch up with history, for somewhere he had lost the sixties to bad times and booze and God knows what sorrow. He would find them, the sixties, after they were over, gathered in a cathedral in New York months later.

The day of my birthday Tennessee asked me to be at his hotel at 9:00 P.M. But my roommate, Jack Weiser, had called from New York and told me that a friend of mine had died of an overdose of speed. It busted me up. I spent the day drinking.

When I returned to the hotel after midnight, I found Tennessee lying on the sofa exhausted, still dressed, a gray hotel blanket thrown over him. Before him on the

all foxlike
and
hunted men

cocktail table was an enormous birthday cake, the candles burned down into the frosting, the edges of it eaten.

"Baby," Tennessee said, "you missed your party. It's over now."

I sat down on the far corner of the sofa and made myself a drink. I looked over at several actors in the room. Everyone was very quiet. I avoided looking at Tennessee because his eyes expressed the disappointment he felt over my nonappearance at the small celebration.

Victor, Tennessee's secretary, came into the room and handed me a list of phone messages. One was from Dave Dellinger. I told Victor I would call him back in the morning.

"You shouldn't drink so much, baby," Tennessee said. It was obvious I was drunk. "How can you stop a war if you're bombed all the time?" The question seemed funny to me: *bombed.* I did not answer.

"Baby," Tennessee said, "these people do not understand revolutionaries. I've always spoken for the oppressed." It was as if knowing my desire to have his cooperation he had devised this little speech to say to me at my birthday party as a gift. The party hadn't happened, so he was saying it now. "And now I've decided to do something. Baby, it's time for me to do something for the movement. It's *past* time! I must speak out! Maybe it's time for the movement to pick up the gun!"

Pick up the gun? The movement couldn't pick up lunch for two at Nedick's.

"We're in trouble, Tenn. I think it'll get a lot worse before it gets any better."

"But the movement will win," he said, trying to counter my depression. "It has *history* with it."

Well, I think what drew Williams to the antiwar movement, what made him accept an invitation to speak at the benefit in December—his first public appearance against the war—and what finally pulled Mailer and Vidal and other writers was a romantic conception of the young and of history itself, the sense that there was an imperative for direct, active participation in the struggles of the left if you were to maintain any credibility among the rising generations.

Sartre had recently said that intellectuals who did not take to the streets in support of workers and students, who stayed at their typewriters, were guilty of "bad faith." He stated, "In my view, the intellectual who does all his fighting from an office is counterrevolutionary today, no matter what he writes." I sensed that was true, that at least some sort of public action was required of the writer beyond his craft, that one's body physically had to be put on the line. However, what kind of action did one undertake?

It seemed increasingly clear to me that demonstrations and legal protests were ineffective and, as the years passed, more and more they seemed exercises in futility and self-indulgence. The benefit that I was organizing, while it might have little or no effect on the war itself, was necessary because it was imperative that the movement get out of debt. People whose freedom depended upon movement resources were in jail. And yet I think I was moving toward the position that a writer was very limited in what he could do with his work once public attitudes on the war had been educated and set, as they were by this time, and that if one had the courage, one had to travel beyond pacific acts to more extreme ones outside the protection of the law, in a word, to violence. And that meant slipping underground and submitting to the discipline of a collective, which necessarily entailed the abandonment of a writer's freedom to write and publish what he wished. One could not work freely knowing that every word directly affected the lives of one's comrades. Obviously, except for polemics and theoretics (for which I had no capacity), one could not be a writer *and* an outlaw, not when the situation demanded obedience to a cadre. The situation in the United States was not comparable to that in France under the Occupation, or in the Soviet Union, where to be a free writer was to be outlaw.

Writers as writers were permitted wide freedom in the United States. Revolutionaries were not. To be a revolutionary meant choosing against the writer. And that I was not prepared to do. So I took half a loaf, rejected Sartre's injunction, and held that fighting through the word was not counterrevolutionary in the United States if one involved oneself to a degree in the public actions of the left. The question then became what degree of involvement was sufficient to exclude bad faith. That I did not know.

It was the avoidance of "bad faith" that made benefits and other public affairs of the left attractive to me as a writer. They allowed you to maintain radical credentials and soothe your conscience without submitting permanently to any collective authority. That had always been the great conflict between writers and the left: How do you solve the dispute between the writer's demand for individual expression, for artistic freedom, and the need for collective organization? It was the inability of the Communist party to resolve that conflict that made it an object of suspicion and contempt on the part of most writers. I shared their contempt for the party. God, it was a painful dilemma, for at the core of it was the hint of elitism—you withdrew, in the name of freedom, part of yourself from the risk and injuries your brothers and sisters, who were not writers, undertook. It was a kind of cheating in the name of a higher good. And that was a source of guilt to me.

Additionally, I believe what attracted Tennessee Williams to the movement was the fact that young people, most especially those committed to media-centered action, provided enormous inputs of creative energy. They made writers feel alive, in contact with history, in a way that books and theater did not. It was important to be well regarded by them. And, of course, there were profound moral and political reasons for the involvement of Williams and Mailer and Vidal and the other writers on the left, however distant that engagement was. Williams especially felt a sense of deep, almost unreasonable solidarity with the victims of oppression. His motives seemed absolutely clean to me. He loved the beaten, the lost, the put-upon, the disregarded, the outsider, the revolutionary. And, as a romantic, the figure of the young man up against it, the young male eager to "pick up the gun," had enormous sexual and emotional appeal to him. When Tennessee spoke of Che he spoke of his beauty. And when he spoke of revolution and of "going to the mountain," I took him quite seriously.

When I asked Tennessee to speak at the benefit on December 6 at the cathedral he agreed enthusiastically. He also, later, wrote a poem for us ("Ripping Off the Mother"), which we sold to *Evergreen Review,* and an article ("We Are Dissenters Now") that was published in *Harper's Bazaar,* the money given to the Peoples Coalition. And during the months preceding the Remember the War Benefit, Tennessee opened himself to wide contact with movement people. He was changed by that experience.

In New York Tennessee and I spent an evening with Abbie Hoffman in his apartment in the Village. Tennessee was anxious to meet Hoffman. Abbie was prominent in the media and I think for that reason Tennessee may have over-rated his importance to the movement. Abbie, while un-questionably an important resource of the left and one of the most celebrated of its media-created leaders, was not central to its actual organizational infrastructure.

Tennessee and Abbie embraced warmly, and Abbie introduced Tennessee to his wife, Anita, who was nursing their new baby, America.

"America!" Tennessee exclaimed. "Baby, you gave him a whole country and all I got's one Southern state!"

We smoked grass and Tennessee drank wine and the hustler-pusher who was with us (my friend) sat stoned on Quaalude on the floor, blond, very young, his face sweaty, perpetually smiling . . . undoing his pink fluff shirt, his hands playing with his nipples; and Tennessee's secretary, Victor, showed Abbie magic tricks, the kind you buy at the toy counter at Woolworth's: a peeper where you look to see a naughty woman and instead get an electric shock, card tricks, mind-reading, kid stuff. . . .

The entire encounter held an element of the absurd, even the pathetic, as Abbie and Tennessee talked of revolution and, later, of Cuba. It was an apparent incongruity to be speaking of revolution while a hustler sat stoned on the floor playing with himself, magic tricks displayed, jokes cracked throughout; but under it, beneath the ego flush Abbie experienced in meeting Tennessee Williams, a celebrity like himself, and beneath the mindlessness of the pot and the Third Avenue sexuality on the floor, was Williams's very real concern to learn where the hell the movement was going, what, in fact, the movement was. And so he came to Abbie Hoffman with a naïveté and a sincere desire to be part of the struggle against imperialism and oppression; a struggle that Abbie Hoffman, accurately or not, through his books and public acts, had come to represent in Tennessee's mind.

It was difficult to get the conversation on a serious level —Abbie's short attention span and his penchant for telling jokes, for entertaining. They talked of Cuba, Tennessee angered by the regime's persecution of homosexuals and writers. It was a question—why intolerance in the revolution?—that Tennessee would ask again and again.

"I met Castro once," Tennessee said. "Oh, in the sixties. Kenneth Tynan got me in to see him. Hemingway was still living in Cuba, you know . . . he gave us a letter, I think. We went to the Palace and waited on the steps for three hours at least. Then we went inside and Castro, what a beautiful man! He *embraced* me! Uhhh, this powerful man, this revolutionary said it was an *honor* to meet *me*. What a gentleman."

Abbie was high, and the two of them exchanged jokes and complimented each other, and Abbie gave Tennessee copies of his books, and we all signed a poster on Abbie's bedroom wall. And it had very little to do with the left or politics, although Tennessee was pleased to be in a room with Abbie Hoffman, seeing in Abbie the streets of Chicago, bombings, resistance, God knows what other symbols of rebellion in the decade, so that he did not notice, or did not mind, the absurdity of the situation. If it was not decadent, that group of us babbling of revolution amidst wine and pot and hustler and the other indulgences of middle-class privilege, it was certainly unserious and most assuredly ironic. We were free men discussing the bondage of others, and getting stoned doing it.

As we were leaving, two May Day types in the blue work shirts and the combat boots who had sat silent throughout the meeting on Abbie's Danish modern couch said, "You bourgeois rip-off artists!"

Tennessee was confused. But then he had a right to be, for his strength, his commitment to the left, was not best seen in his life and his personal enthusiasm but in his art. So he rose on the balls of his feet and said, defensively, "Abbie's a *saint!* Such courage. Magnificent. He's accepted his death. He's been to the mountain!"

"I don't wanna die!" Abbie wailed. "I don't wanna die!"

"You've been to the mountain, baby," Tennessee said, correcting Abbie. He said it sadly.

All that night Tennessee rode high on the encounter with Abbie Hoffman, for it was to him an encounter with the history of the New Left. Of course, it was nothing of the kind. Late at night we stood in a parking lot in the East Village after having been to a show and a saloon. Tennessee and I pissed against a wall, Tennessee singing at the top of his lungs, "Mary, sweeter than you know. . . ." And I pointed out the graffiti sprayed on the wall: ROCKEFELLER MURDERER! AVENGE ATTICA! That was reality, not the meeting with Abbie. Attica was what the left was about.

Tennessee said, "God bless the movement!" and then shyly, "Off the pigs!" He was learning the argot.

I took Tennessee to a demonstration against the Attica Prison massacre. We waited at Rockefeller Center with Betty Peterson, Dave Dellinger's wife, for the demonstrators to arrive from Union Square. As the leading pacifist in the United States and the chief organizer of the antiwar movement, Dellinger had spoken downtown, attempting to marshal the moral force of the movement against the murders at Attica. At that time we believed that Attica was the beginning of a more widespread government employment of raw violence against any dissent. That it had been ordered by an alleged "liberal" governor only made it appear more ominous in our eyes.

Finally the demonstrators reached us. People in the line of march recognized Tennessee and raised their fists in greeting. He returned the salute. It was two days after Attica. And we understood that afternoon that the movement's ability to attract people into the streets had diminished enormously; expecting ten thousand marchers, we pulled less than eight hundred. We waited for Dave Dellinger, who was bringing up the rear of the march, plodding along at the end in his rumpled beige tweed jacket and brown corduroy trousers, carrying a package of books under his arm. He had brought along copies of his book *"Revolutionary Non-violence"* for Tennessee and me.

"Dave!" I yelled happily, and he jogged over grinning, embraced Betty, and then threw his arms around Tennessee and me.

We strolled through the crowd of demonstrators on Fifty-Second Street decrying Nelson Rockefeller as an assassin, and while the speeches droned on I pointed out to Tennessee various friends in the crowd, among them former Weatherman Brian Flanagan in a floppy tan pimp's hat, lifting his fist and grinning his Irish grin. He had been tried for attempted murder in the paralyzing of Mayor Daley's counsel Elrod during the Weatherman "Days of Rage," when I had run with them in the streets seeing revolution in every broken window and bleeding face. Brian had been acquitted. "He looks Irish," Tennessee said. "When I was young the Irish became cops."

Then Julian Beck and his wife, Judith Malina, came over, hugging everybody, all of us astonished to find them there, none of us having known they had returned from imprisonment in Brazil.

Betty, Judith and Julian, Dave, Tennessee, and I left the demonstration, joined by Tom Seligson, the writer. We ended up at a bar in the RCA building.

Tennessee was in high spirits, we all were, and he kept mugging, laughing loudly, cracking jokes. We were all together after a protest, united by friendship and by a common hatred for institutions we saw as a common enemy, believing that we believed as one, that we had all paid out in different measure enough to command unity from each other.

Williams asked Judith Malina, "How bad was it, baby?" referring to their imprisonment in Brazil.

"It was unbelievable. We requested a room for the company to rehearse in at the prison." That seemed to me an odd request, perhaps not utterly appropriate to the situation, but I said nothing and Judith continued talking very quietly, twisting a napkin between her fingers. She spoke so softly that we leaned forward to hear her, Dellinger cupping his ear. She told her story dramatically.

"They gave the room to us. It was next to the one in which they tortured the men. We could hear them screaming, political prisoners, young, young men screaming and crying as we tried to rehearse a theater piece in the next room. Oh, my God, it was . . ." She started to cry, sniffling and coughing, and while I was moved by her tears, I could not understand why anybody would want to rehearse in prison and then be surprised when the sadists running the can put them next to a torture room. The entire thing seemed other-worldly, indeed almost frivolous, if one did not appreciate the passion or singlemindedness the Becks brought to the theater.

Judith went on about their experiences in Brazil, about Julian being beaten and thrown down a flight of stairs by the guards after questioning. I don't know, there was something about her, her black hair and wild dark eyes, the refusal to give way to age, her tininess and insistent sexuality, which gave her an implacability like that of Edith Piaf or some aging beauty who plays to our sentimentality, who has spent a lifetime watching her beauty pass and die in third-rate provincial playhouses, crying, with mascara running down her cheeks, and it was that sense I had of her as an obsessive personality when it came to the theater which allowed me to take seriously her remarks about rehearsing in jail while people were tortured. It was quite mad, but then who was I to judge, when I had not experienced what she had of Brazil and the jails and the loss.

Later, we returned to the subject of Cuba. I asked Dave Dellinger how often he had seen Castro.

"I've been there five or six times." Dellinger leaned forward on the table, his scotch-on-the-rocks in front of him, gripping a large cigar between his fingers. He was smiling slightly. One of the characteristics of his style was the surprise he evidenced when you asked him a friendly question about himself: he lit up, grinning (You really want to know about me?). It was a spontaneous reaction I have seen many times with him. It was part of what drew one to him, his humility. "Castro's always late. I've waited in the hotel in Havana more than a day for him, with his people constantly making frantic calls to me saying one thing or another delays his arrival. Some crisis holds him up."

"But what about the arts there?" Williams asked rhetorically. "And what's the role of art in revolution, of the artist, baby?" He took Judith's hand, speaking intensely, dramatically. *"It's to do what he does best!"* He grunted. Enough said. "To do his *work.*"

His work? Well, work was life to Tennessee. It defined his will. It was what he was about. He was the only writer I knew who worked every single day. I spent evenings drinking late with him, sleeping until noon, while he rose at dawn and made coffee and went to the typewriter and began life again. He was like a fisherman whose life was little more than catching fish, who smelled of them, knew the feel of their bodies as he knew the texture of his hands. And that chore of fishing, that constant intimacy with his prey, was the fisherman's only disciplined passion. Words were Tennessee's fish. And if the fish died out?

Dellinger interrupted Williams. "There are two tendencies in Cuba. The bureaucratic socialists aligned with the Soviet Union, they are repressive of the arts and of homosexuals, of sexual liberation in general. And then there are—"

"What does it *matter!*" Tennessee was being histrionic. He was having no part of this explanation.

"It does. The other tendency is Fidel's," Dellinger continued, "which is open to experimentation. For a while the arts flowered in Cuba."

Seligson spoke up: "But unlike the state, the arts wither away."

Tennessee looked at Tom. "Uhhh . . . what is the importance of art?" he said. The remark was sad rather than cynical.

"It has *great* value."

"How can you place *value* on *art,*" Tennessee flared, "when there are *guns pointed at your country's throat!*" He jabbed at his throat with his hand. *"The missiles!* The Soviet, the Cubans, they are *surrounded,* baby, *they are under siege!* There are more important things than art. When the imperialists have you surrounded—"

"Tennessee . . ." Dave tried to interrupt. Tennessee was

outflanking him on the left. I jumped in. "It's *social fascist,* Tenn, what the Cubans and Soviets do to homosexuals and artists."

Dellinger: "It's *bureaucratic* socialist." We were both trying to think up some label to apply to official intolerance in a socialist state to remove it from our conceptions of true socialism. Everything socialist was good. The bad was something else entirely. All excesses can be explained. But what we did not understand was that Tennessee did not give a damn, he had no need of explanation. He went ahead with his defense of the revolution while we, somewhat ridiculously, attempted to make too precise definitions to mitigate revolutionary responsibility for crimes.

Tennessee, turning on me: "What do you expect? *The revolution isn't won!*"

"No, it's *betrayed!*"

"They are *encircled,* baby!"

"Betrayed! Betrayed!" I was shouting.

"It takes time, baby." And then, as if echoing my thoughts that it was presumptuous of us to debate the correctness of the Cuban experiment, he said, "Who are we to judge?" He was being absolutely sincere. "They think us decadent. Dissipated. *Look* at yourself." He was speaking to me, waving his hand theatrically. "Just *look.* As artists and revolutionaries your task is to do your work. To make art, baby. Who are we to *judge* the men who *die* . . . But I will go to the mountain. I have gone before, Dotson, many times."

Two days after the Attica demonstrations I had dinner with Tennessee at his hotel in Manhattan. After dinner we took a walk along the East Side. I bought Tennessee some daffodils on Third Avenue near the hotel. He was down. I think he missed Dellinger and the others, for, with Dave anyway, he felt in contact with something real and future, something with which connection had been broken years before. Through Dellinger and others he was communicating again with what he understood as youth, as future, as new life, as rebellion and revolution.

He once asked Dellinger if he was a Communist.

"Not with a capital C. I think of myself as an anarchist-socialist. Lenin said the state would wither away—"

Tennessee: "Lovely. *Wither away* . . ."

"—and in time you could build a communist society, true liberty. I am a libertarian socialist."

Tennessee thought a moment. "I am a socialist, too. A revolutionary and an artist. I renounce death! Ha! I *live!*"

And this: in November, weeks before the benefit at the cathedral, Tennessee returned to New York from Rome, where he had seen Gore Vidal.

In December Vidal was to tell me that he no longer recognized Williams. "We've been friends a long time. He's changed. And you haven't helped any, Dotson, leading him down the garden path. *He doesn't know anything about politics!* For Christ's sake, you've filled his head with a lot of radical crap."

Tennessee and I had lunch at a pancake palace near his hotel. He talked about Rome for a time and about his desire someday to buy a small farm in Italy ("a few goats and geese") and settle there. And then he spoke of seeing Vidal in Rome, and of what Vidal had told him.

"Gore said I shouldn't trust you, Dotson, that you're irresponsible. That you're leading me on, baby. He said he knows you well." Tennessee narrowed his eyes, and repeated, "*He knows you well.*"

"I never met the man." I had not then, and when I did meet Vidal in December it was under appropriate circumstances: at the *Screw* magazine anniversary party at Max's Kansas City bar where Vidal received a bronzed statuette in the shape of a penis for his political work.

"That you try—"

"I never met the man."

"It doesn't matter," he said, not believing me. "Revolutionaries have to use any means. Even their best friends. Revolutionaries are fugitives."

Maybe. Foxlike and hunted men. Hell, I was not a revolutionary. I had not the guts, even though I ached to see the spark, the flush that, for one pulse beat, let the land leap fishlike from the net of dark. Maybe that "ache" was sentimentality, cheap romanticism, or maybe it was a sexual hunger that was confused in my mind with political causes. I did not care. It was one of the few things I owned that I had any pride in.

5

The fall and winter of 1971 were difficult times for the movement. The Evict Nixon demonstrations in Washington, organized by the Peoples Coalition largely through the Washington-based May Day Tribe (the loose grouping of hippies, ex-Weatherpeople, crazies, Yippies, former SDS cadres gathered around Rennie Davis), were a fiasco. We had announced that tens of thousands of protesters would take to the streets in a bigger-than-life repeat of the May Day demonstrations. Who appeared? About eight hundred rain-soaked protestors, May Day people joined by the Old Guard in a sort of rehearsal reunion before the Big Bash senior prom at the Cathedral of St. John the Divine: Tom Hayden, Dellinger, Seligson, Ed Sanders, John Froines, Stu Alpert, Jerry Rubin, Father Groppi, even a few CP types.

I was in Washington a week, longer than I had planned. The delay was caused by the rain, and by our continually postponing the final action as we waited for the expected demonstrators to appear. Finally, when we realized that as the days passed our numbers diminished rather than grew, we scheduled our civil disobedience for Pennsylvania Avenue.

About three hundred of us were arrested sitting in the avenue by the Treasury Building, sitting there in the intersection stopping traffic while rookie police got their rocks off ramming their motor scooters into us. Dellinger

*the
whole
world
is watching*

and Rennie leading us, we shouted, *"The whole world is watching!"* Practically no one was. Our great fall offensive against the war was a rain-out, a disaster. Dave Dellinger and I didn't even have money for our bail. Tennessee had to be called to send us bail.

In the face of the October failure, our last major "action" of the year, the coming Cathedral benefit—which I was now permanently charged with organizing—loomed more and more important. It had to be a success, financially and in terms of public relations. For we desperately needed a success, needed the energy and the renewal of support a massive public achievement would provide.

Twice Rennie Davis came up from Washington to meet with Dave Dellinger, McReynolds, Seligson, and me at my apartment where we talked long into the night, all of us drinking heavily, trying to think through the incredible indebtedness and the blackout on media coverage which confronted the movement . . . all of us drinking, that is, except Rennie, who sat on the floor, his knees up, his elbows resting on them, his head against his hands, saying very little, showing no enthusiasm. Rennie was one of the two or three finest organizers in the antiwar movement. And he was handsome to women, resembling Peter Fonda more than a little. Yet he made me uncomfortable. His silence was too complete. I did not then know the particulars of some of the more exotic infighting within the movement, much of it along generational not ideological lines, although even there divisions obviously nonideological in basis were always articulated in complex political terms. I had heard enough to know that Rennie was at the bottom of many of them. And my own experience with him and his allies was a difficult one. It seemed to me that he acted to divide the Coalition and, if he did not in fact establish a competitive organization outside of it, his May Day grouping effectively acted as such within it. Dellinger, unlike Rennie Davis, strove to keep things together. It was a thankless task.

One other point about Rennie: he elicited fierce loyalty

from his friends. And he rarely acted directly. One saw the results of his moves, of his planning, but one could not trace their history. Perhaps that is because he appeared to move mainly by telephone (a very New York vice) and avoided the face-to-face kind of public battle most movement people engaged in with a relish in their organizational meetings. I guess he differed from most of us in that he acted more like a revolutionary than like a reform Democrat.

At the last meeting with Rennie at my apartment it was agreed to set up a benefit office and to staff it. I was to be given "seed money" to pay staff expenses (neither Seligson nor I were on the payroll). In the end, of course, no money was forthcoming and we had to raise it ourselves.

Much of the final meeting was taken up in a long argument over what two new staff members were to be paid. I said a hundred a week apiece. Dave McReynolds held out for thirty-eight dollars a week, which he claimed was the traditional starting pay for functionaries.

"That's what I started out with. It took me ten years to work myself up to seventy-five dollars a week."

Such were the movement's Civil Service regulations. We finally compromised. They would receive eighty dollars a week. The first money crisis was over.

Beginning in September I became a functionary behind an old wooden desk at Peoples Coalition headquarters in the garment district, trying to organize a benefit with one hand while coping with the obscure, gritty, neurotic, petulant, loony, internal politics of the antiwar movement with the other.

We needed sixty thousand dollars to get the Coalition out of hock. It was important that the Coalition survive, for it was the largest antiwar organization in America, an alliance of fifty national groups: Women Strike for Peace, Vietnam Veterans Against the War, the Vietnam Peace Parade Committee, the War Resisters League, the Communist party, Quakers, National Welfare Rights Organization, etc. It was what remained of the nominally democratic, non-Trotskyist left in the United States.

Our chief competitor for dominance of the antiwar movement was the National Peace Action Coalition—Student Mobilization Committee (NPAC–SMC), which we spent a lot of time struggling against because it was Trotskyist and therefore, in our eyes, counterrevolutionary. It was a front organization dominated by the Socialist Workers party, an offshoot of the Communist party, which attacked the party for being "revisionist and bourgeois." These two coalitions, then, the democratic left (with the CP arranged under that title, although its commitment to democratic principles was questionable) and the Trots, contended for hegemony over the movement against imperialism and racism in America.

While everyone in the antiwar movement was part of it because of a deep, abiding outrage over the immorality of that conflict, some of us saw the war as the commanding organizational tool at our disposal.

If you were radical, one of the things you were dedicated to was subversion. That is obvious. Thus, you had occasion to champion a lot of things that had no direct relationship to yourself, some of which you didn't even like, because those things were subversive to the established system of values. Certainly in the sixties we were involved in the creation of alternative systems of values and alternative institutions and ways of living to counter established order and values to which we were opposed. For example, I defended the legalization of pot, state heroin maintenance, homosexuality and other deviate behavior, the abolition of prisons, and so forth not because they were necessarily appealing to me (I do not especially like pot; it makes my mouth dry) but rather because I knew that in championing them one acted against the political order that suppressed them. One worked to politicize everything, to champion and promote all activity by the young which divided them from the system. We worked, quite properly, to sow distrust of the government, of all institutions. And if you were a radical writer you were revolutionary to the degree that your work was subversive, i.e., functioned to radicalize its readers.

We reasoned that all outlaws (I use that term in its simplest, least theatrical sense) were by definition on the side of revolution. They were legally labeled outsiders. They had less to lose and more to gain by radical changes in the social order. By this reasoning I could see how homosexuals, lesbians, drug addicts, freaks, prisoners, deserters, nonbelievers, women seeking illegal abortions, people practicing nonconformist sexual acts, truants, delinquents, and so forth all were our natural allies. The criminal classes and the *lumpenproletariat,* in short, were the class base. The task was to make them realize it, make them understand that acid and homosexuality and shooting a landlord could all be political acts.

Let me digress a moment and take the figure of the homosexual as an example. I choose him for several reasons: of the various militancies on the left, the one with which I had the least visceral sympathy was gay liberation and yet it was the one I understood well because it was like all outsiders, like me, concerned with human freedom and with the establishment of personhood (in this instance manhood) in the most desperate terms.

A few years ago I witnessed a gay liberation demonstration in front of the Women's House of Detention in Greenwich Village. It was the conclusion of a march from Times Square that night by about three hundred supporters of homosexual rights. In the Village traffic was stopped and about two thousand people lined the streets out of curiosity or in support of the homosexual protest. I don't need to say that the homosexual youth looked like any other American youth, that they were intent to hold their ground, to stand, and their determination gave to them as individuals a dignity that was handsome. As the crowd chanted, women prisoners in the House of Detention began dropping burning slips of paper from the windows down upon the police below. The crowd cheered. Police reinforcements arrived, and the bloodletting commenced.

It was at this juncture, when the crowd was hurling bottles and cans at the police, and the police were charging into the people, pulling young men from the crowd and stick-whipping them about the face and groin, that I arrived on the scene. And my response was a kind of horrified fascination. Not over the brutality of the police, for I had been through enough police riots and busts to realize how commonplace violence was; rather, my interest was held by the attitude of the police in this situation as distinct from their attitude in other situations where they attempted "crowd control." There was something in their manner, a sexual arrogance in their mistreatment of the homosexuals, an undisguised contempt that was different from the disdain I had come to expect from them in confrontations where their political and class biases were manifested. It was different from antiwar demonstrations, from standard leftist political street actions. Their response to the gays was deeper, more profound, less rational, housed more intimately in their subconscious, beyond articulation, as if they were responding to a threat personified by the homosexuals which was more personal in character and hence more dangerous than that advanced by leftists in the streets. It was as personal, as individualistic, and as unstructured as a barroom brawl; a response equal to, and of the same quality as, the response of booze-dizzy straights to homosexuals when they take it into mind to go fag-rolling. It was that ambiguous—and that vulgar. It was degenerate. And what was startling to me was that while I politically supported the homosexual activists, I found myself emotionally siding with the police. I shared their contempt for the homosexual. I did not know how to explain that, whether it was because these homosexuals being up front, out in the streets, in some way were threatening to my sexuality, more threatening than the police, or because I held some secret bias against homosexuals arising from my early days in New York when I was broke and often resorted to them as sources of money and in the payment received humiliation and abuse as gratuity. Perhaps it was deeper than that, a resentment coming from my belief that they cheapened life because they were antipathetic to creation. In fellatio and pederasty I saw not only self-indulgence, the avoidance of responsibility (and if there was a blanket crime characteristic of the age it was the irresponsibility of all classes in this civilization), but also the murder of seed. Homosexuality was not an act of life. It was death in sexuality; it was the murder of potential life in the name of pleasure.

While I had always felt deep sympathy for the social position of the homosexual (anger over official discrimination against them) and knew that there was a direct ratio between the effeminacy of the individual gay and the degree of my concern (queens were no threat, and thus I could become deeply moved by their sadness), it was witnessing *organized* homosexuals acting militantly in the street *as* homosexuals which was decidedly upsetting to me. They were there like all other militant outsiders before them, seeking their rights, and thus had claim on my concern, and still I hesitated.

Even my reaction to the violence was bewilderment, for the event was unmapped. That is, I owned no key to my own feelings. It was difficult to chart a sexual demonstration with political pretenses. It was as if one were witnessing a dirty mob fight after a football game between supporters of two rival high-school teams, only in this situation one side dressed as cops, the other as street people. My reaction to it was on that level, that it was not quite serious, not political. It should not have occurred, neither the demonstration nor the violence.

However, I was wrong. It should have occurred. The homosexual element in the United States, in northern Europe, in Cuba, and most other socialist countries generally was a brutalized and mutilated minority, and their persecution was without justification, although not without reason.

The motivation behind antihomosexual discrimination, on a personal level, was confused and obscure to me, and I could not hope to fathom reasons as recondite and elemental as those underlying the straight male's distaste for and distrust and fear of homosexuals. Nevertheless, on an official level, discrimination against homosexuals was understandable. It was a defensive response to the most subversive of forces: those which attacked the organization and purpose of society and its fundamental ordering unit, the nuclear family. It was here, in hostility to the nuclear family, in the rejection of creation (life) in sexuality, the rejection of socially ordered heterosexual pairing as the primary vehicle for the conveyance of societal tradition and the internalization of morality, that the gay liberation and the women's liberation movements (which I believed were essentially antagonistic) came together. It was precisely for that reason that I, regardless of personal prejudice, had to support the homosexual's struggle; because, like women's liberation, the homosexual movement understood the nuclear family as a mechanism of oppression, a device by which institutionalized heterosexuality, and the values which sustained it, was manipulated to ensure the supremacy of the dominant male. In attacking the nuclear family—and every pedication between males was such an attack—the gay liberation movement authenticated, however obliquely, its revolutionary purposes and embodied its threat to the commanding social, economic, and political arrangements. The revolutionary nature of homosexual rebellion was obvious to communists like the Weatherman, who self-consciously encouraged intrasexuality in their communes as a means of building solidarity, of vitiating bourgeois individualism and countering intersexual competition with women as sexual trophies, of exposing and destroying male chauvinism and privilege and, lastly, of creating a brotherhood of humiliation. If a male heterosexual (and among white, male heterosexuals perhaps the most given to machismo was the self-regarding revolutionary youth) could be made to face and embrace a terror as deeply rooted and threatening as homosexuality in the name of the revolution, then what, in God's name, would he not do? Homosexuality became perversely for heterosexual youth a process of voluntary brutalization and conversion, an instrument for the creating of subversives.

And that takes me back to the role of the left as a subversive force. Ridicule, contempt, distrust directed against institutions were means to set the climate for radicalization. But the war was the chief means we had to radicalize the young. It provided the young, who were naturally rebellious of authority—most especially young males, fifteen to twenty years old, who were our main constituency—with a concrete enemy, someone to side against. Once they understood that the government was actually willing to kill them to maintain capitalist influence in Indochina seven thousand miles away, that was threat enough. Demonstrations, beatings by police, tear gas functioned dramatically and effectively to *convert* (in its religious sense) the young overnight, to make them radical. As soon as the national government was perceived as the enemy, it was relatively easy to teach them to see the police as their enemy, and schoolteachers and university administrators, parents, bosses, shopkeepers, anyone who was in authority or was part of the privileged classes. We knew we would never win a majority to our side. But then a revolution does not need a majority.

Again, the war was essential to the process. And that was why the left struggled endlessly with itself over which tendency in the antiwar movement would emerge in control over the issue of the war.

And, of course, as I was just beginning to see, my own role in this movement was paradoxical. I understood where its most militant section was headed. I knew that when revolution came to America (and I still believe it is coming, although somewhat delayed) I would be among the class it would liquidate. It would have to. Because once it was established in authority, the revolution would be the enemy. And I would not submit.

We were, as I have noted, going through hard times on the left, harder than usual. To a significant degree, Nixon had temporarily defused the war in Indochina as a political issue, and the companion issues of racism and domestic oppression proved to be difficult ones for mass organization. In terms of national issues what we had, as I said, was the war and that had quieted down as a result of "Vietnamization." We knew Vietnamization would not work in the long run. Therefore, our task was to ensure the survival of the Peoples Coalition until the following spring, when new offensives in Indochina or domestic political developments—*something*—would again give us the political means to stage what we hoped would be the final peace offensive against Nixon and the war. We had to survive until the 1972 elections. To do that we needed money. And to get money we had to resurrect our public image as a reputable, responsible political movement. The Remember the War Benefit on December 6 became essential to those ends.

Knowing the importance of the benefit, we expected enthusiastic support from the several organizations within the Coalition. Instead we found ourselves in premature fights over how the nonexistent profits would be divided, arguments over program, advertising, advertising copy, over the use of outside professionals. In short, argument over everything.

On professionals: we (Rennie Davis, Dave Dellinger, William Douthard and Norma Becker of the Vietnam Peace Parade Committee, and, most important, Tom Seligson) had decided to enlist "nonmovement" professionals to handle as much of the actual work as possible. Thus, Jerry Murff and Howard Rosenman at Benton and Bowles contributed the design of advertising and radio promotion. The printing was donated. Radio ads were taped free by professional studios.

Through Bishop Paul Moore of New York we acquired use of the Cathedral of St. John the Divine. That was important: it was the largest hall in Manhattan outside of Madison Square Garden; it gave us a considerable amount of much needed respectability since it was the premier see of the Episcopal Church; and it offered us, we thought, the best situation in terms of security, something we were very worried about.

I think it was, in part, the fact that we would be in the cathedral that finally coaxed Norman Mailer into coming aboard. The idea of performing his play *D.J.* before the high altar was too good to resist, considering his view of the world.

"I'm Satan," he said, when we discussed having the play performed.

"So am I," I replied, not willing to give him such an illustrious identity.

"No, you're only *half* Satan."

Half a loaf is better than none.

One of the purposes of the benefit was to garner new respectability for the antiwar movement and to break the press blackout on our activities. We hoped to overcome the media view of us as wild-eyed fanatics trashing the streets of Washington. Therefore, we decided to set up a letterhead committee to act as sponsor of the benefit, a committee composed of as many notables as possible who were not already associated in the public's mind with the Peoples Coalition.

We created a public fiction: the Benefit Committee for the Peoples Coalition for Peace and Justice. Dave Dellinger was chairman; Dave McReynolds and myself, vice chairmen; Tom Seligson, treasurer; Cora Weiss, of the Committee of Liaison with Families of American Soldiers Detained in Vietnam, secretary. The actual organizational work was done by Tom Seligson and me.

The Committee members were: Julian Beck, Malcolm Boyd, Jimmy Breslin, Ossie Davis, Rennie Davis, Willem de

Kooning, Martin Duberman, Jules Feiffer, Ruth Ford, Paul Goodman, Nat Hentoff, Norman Mailer, Bishop Paul Moore, Jack Newfield, Richard Poirier, Susan Sontag, Gloria Steinem, and Tennessee Williams.

That was it. We were in business.

6

Six people refused to join the Benefit Committee. Lillian Hellman did not want to join any letterhead committees when she had not the time or the energy to be actively involved. She wished us luck. John and Yoko Lennon, who could never make up their minds. And Andy Warhol, Germaine Greer, and Abbie Hoffman. Their refusals were very interesting. The three of them, like the others, we asked to participate primarily because we wanted as widely representative a body of people as we could find on the committee. And they each had different talents that would have been valuable to us.

I think I was most interested in getting Warhol involved in the benefit and, through it, in the movement against the war. I had known him since 1965 or 1966. We shared similar psychological responses to violence. And I admired him. So I wanted him with me.

I met him during the period of the flower children in the East Village when drugs and life were compatible and we did not know, had no idea, of what it would cost us, this drug romance, in the years ahead, payment made with the sanity and lives of some of our friends.

I began seeing more of him; I hung around the Factory (his studio on Union Square), and Max's and other bars where his friends and people connected with the Theatre of the Ridiculous and La Mama, actors, artists, writers, and others young and unknown, built a kind of community

perverse
chic

and affection that sustained them for a while. We thought it would go on forever, the underground. It died. I think of drugs.

In October 1971 I saw Warhol alone. I knew if I asked him to aid any left-wing cause while his manager-director Paul Morrissey was around I would get nowhere. Morrissey had the political mentality of President Harding. He yearned for a return to normalcy, a state he visualized in terms of Hollywood musicals circa 1946. Also, Warhol's politics being none too substantial, I wanted to be able to explain slowly and carefully what we were about. I do not think he understood, in an ideological way, anything of what had occurred in the world during the last ten years, although his gut responses were true. Certainly, in the *Velvet Underground* and the *Exploding Plastic Inevitable,* in the disaster paintings, in his films beatifying manhood through violence, through the cult of leather, with his bikeboys and hustlers and impotent studs worn through and fazing out on scag and the pretenses of the butch, in that vision he joined with much of what rumbled in the consciousness of the New Left, much of what was true for the Weatherman and the Panther and, for a time, true for me. He knew how to manipulate and celebrate Perverse Chic, which was, contrary to Tom Wolfe's understanding, the essential definition of radical-social politics in New York.

One afternoon in the spring, Andy and I left the Factory and crossed the park to Park Avenue South to get a taxi. As we left the park about fifteen youths, Trotskyists who do not like me, saw Andy and me, or at least they saw *me,* for they started running in our direction, raising their fists in the air and shouting curses. They were very angry, and Andy pulled close to me, said nothing, simply gripped my arm and drew himself near, peeking around me at the youths running in the park toward us and shouting. The boys stopped abruptly on the other side of the street, yelled a few more curses, and ran away.

Warhol and I got a taxi. He said nothing, nothing in the

taxi, nothing when we arrived at a party later. Nothing, that is, about the Trots cursing in the park. And then much later, suddenly, he asked me, as if recalling something urgent, "Who . . . who was the boy in leather? You know, all in brown leather?"

I looked at him oddly, I was into more than a few drinks and I was baffled by the question, for it had nothing to do with what was at hand, pertinent not at all to what we had been talking about. And it was asked with such shyness, awkwardly, half-embarrassed.

"*What* boy?"

"In the park," he said. "The boy running in the park. He had on leather pants. And a leather jacket . . . it was *brown* leather. It was *neat.*"

"So what if he had leather on?"

"But it was so *neat,*" Andy said softly. "I think he was so neat." Well, I think it was the leather and the probability of violence that he understood as neat. The boy running through Union Square past the Factory next to which stood the burned-out quarters of the Black Panther Defense Committee bombed weeks before. If Warhol did not understand politics, he understood the urgency of violence and its sexual character. That was enough.

I asked him to serve on the Committee. "I have to ask Paul," he said.

"But Paul's a reactionary! He'll say no!"

"I don't know anything about politics. And that's so old-fashioned, politics and stuff. This is the seventies."

"But it's just a dummy committee. We want your name, Andy. For the stationery. You don't have to *pay* anything." Andy was terribly tight with his money.

"Oh, I don't know. Uh, maybe I could do something else?"

"What about doing a radio commercial for us."

"I can't talk."

"But Gore Vidal is doing one."

"Really?"

"And Tony Perkins."

"Oh, really?"

"And Ruth Ford."

"Ruth Ford is doing one?"

"And Rex Reed and Susan Sontag."

"Susan Sontag?" He was confused. "But she's a writer, isn't she?"

"Sure. Everybody's doing them. It's such fun we have to turn people away, Andy."

"Uh, well, maybe Joe could do it and you could say it's me. Or Candy Darling. Candy would be *wonderful*."

He never did the commercial. But he and his superstars were at the benefit, along with the Cockettes and a gathering of drag queens dropping sequins and leather boys smelling of Old Spice. *That* part of the decade would not miss the show. They came, like the rest of us, to drop their beads one last time. And Andy stood in the back of the Cathedral, his Catholic mind reeling at the dirty words used in Mailer's play before the high altar, and the kids smoking pot. In *church!* "It's just like . . . uh, you know . . . it's just like the Dom [a discothèque] used to be. Like the *sixties*. It's *fabulous*."

I spent days calling Germaine Greer at the Chelsea Hotel and getting noncommittal answers. Finally, Tom Seligson and I confronted her over dinner one night in a seedy artist's loft in Soho. Germaine entered into bitter argument concerning Norman Mailer. There was no chance for us. When I asked her to join the Committee, she would not. "I wouldn't be on *any* fucking thing . . . I wouldn't be on a bloody *lifeboat* with that—!"

Finally, Abbie Hoffman's refusal. . . . Several weeks before the Benefit Committee was completed, sometime in late November, Tennessee Williams and I went down to Rip Torn's house in Chelsea to visit his wife, Geraldine Page, and also, for my part, to discuss the benefit with Abbie. We had not seen him since the evening at his apartment months before.

The night at Torn's was a downer. Abbie told Tennessee, who was beginning to suffer some prebenefit jitters, that he had had it with the movement. "I ain't going to be around for the benefit. I ain't even going to be around for the conventions. Shit, no! They ain't going to pin *that* on me, not this time. They beat me up enough, broke my nose, busted my back. I don't like *pain*, Tennessee. I want to *live,* man. Me and Anita, we're going somewhere warm. We leave the streets to you people."

What Abbie said depressed Tennessee. It depressed me. Tennessee did not know how to respond. He went upstairs to see Geraldine Page.

Alone, Abbie said to me, in reply to my asking his help on the benefit weeks away, "This benefit is crazy, Dotson. That shit don't work no more. Don't be so fucking dumb."

We passed around a joint.

Abbie: "You seen old Gus lately? You still pal around with old Gus? Ha! Ha!"

"Nope."

"You know, those Commies, they're pretty *old.*" Abbie shook his head, reflecting on the image.

"I think I'll end up like old Gus."

Abbie howled. "You got to be kidding! Didn't you tell me that before? Ha! Shit, man, *nobody* ends like Gus! Nobody's *that* old! Wow, that's boring, man. All they're interested in is good plumbing. That's what the Commies want. When me and Anita were in Yugoslavia, that's what they showed us, *plumbing.* When we arrived in Rome we saw *Satyricon,* and I turned to Anita and said, 'God, give us *decadence!'* It ain't boring anyway. But the Commies. . . ." Abbie shivered. "Man, what do they got you want? Huh? They got *cards.* You ever *seen* them cards, huh? They *say* they got cards, but nobody ever seen them cards they carry. Man, did you ever see them cards?"

I tried once more. "We need you on the Committee, Abbie."

"I'm getting old."

"Think of the future, of the movement!"

He reflected a moment, growing serious. He *was* down that night. "My kids dropped out of school. I got a ten-year-old kid who won't *listen* to *reason!* Ha! Like in the last two weeks we sort of had a *serious discussion.* Ha! I mean but finally I agree with them, with everything that they were laying down. They're now going to school where somebody started a day school, somebody who digs kids and gathered all these kids like a pied piper gathers them. Takes the kids to this school with a computer. Like, my ten-year-old can't read and write so good and here he is fucking winging it with a *computer.* And I'm just looking at it, like, holy shit! I think at that point I felt old a little. I felt grown up. I really felt that maybe there was——"

"We're all grown up. Ain't it hell."

"But when you start talking to kids brought up on the new math and computers, wow. I think their chief characteristic is noncompetitiveness. My kids just . . . they don't *compete.* And if you, like, try to bribe them, well, like, 'the other kids can do that, and Charlie can do that, Andy [his son], why can't, why can't you?' And you give him that *look,* you know, that's supposed to *sink.* They just don't accept that. They won't accept that kind of jive. Big deal. They think, so big deal . . . Every winter I think, what am I doing here, you know? I don't know . . ."

Abbie left, telling me he was going to a Florida beach and sit with fat, blue-haired Jewish ladies having nose jobs and try to figure out what the hell happened to all of us.

"The sixties, like, they came so fast. Bang! Wham! Zowie! We don't even know what hit us. We're still spinning. We got to figure out what the hell we are and what the fucking future is. Can't play the same shitty games no more. It ain't in giving benefits, Dotson, it ain't there. We're freaks. That's what we are. *Freaks! Freaks!* Far out, man. Weird. Like, I don't even understand my oldest boy when he talks. He's way ahead of me. The movement's finished. It's *weirds-ville*. It's over."

Later, at Tennessee's hotel we had drinks with Jann Eller, who was now going to trial, facing imprisonment of two years to life. He was twenty-five years old. I had first met him in Chicago in July 1969, when we were both delegates to the last national SDS convention. Then he was unbelievably naïve, innocent if you will. He did not understand the meanings of common words, had no sense of duplicity in gesture or tone, no ability whatsoever to sense a threat that was not obvious and unambiguous.

Jann had shared a room at the Y in Chicago with me and Eric Mann (head of the Weatherman in Boston). He lay on the floor on the mattress and I was above him on the bed, and at night I lay and looked down at him, his hair wet from a bath, the room dark, and his yellow hair shiny in the light from the bathroom. One day, outside on Madison in Chicago, I stopped him in the street and told him not to move, in the middle of the intersection with the traffic roaring, and let me look at him a moment, for the sunshine was on his eyes, blue-green, and the sun penetrated so deeply, like a jungle trail, like a pool . . . I am out of images. It was beauty and I wanted it to remain in the sunlight a time so I would remember it. What attracted me there, pulled tenderness from me to him like cotton drawn from a boll, what made me want to protect him, was the feeling that he was fated to die violently, that he stood vulnerable to the dread milling sharply about him and that he was unaware. I have remembered.

So that night with Tennessee, Jann was on his way back to the Coast to begin gathering together his defense. He was being tried for assaulting a police officer in a demonstration against the war.

We talked about Abbie and what he had said earlier, about the death of the movement. None of us really accepted that assessment, certainly not Tennessee, when it implied that this handsome gentle man about to stand trial had expended his future on a movement that was not of the future but of the past. It was nearly impossible to accept. And yet the suspicion remained.

"This country's mad," Tennessee said, "and I don't know what good the benefit will do. Will it get this child out of prison? Will it stop the war?"

He paused, and I was reminded of Mailer's skepticism, and then Tennessee continued, "I don't know, baby. Maybe Abbie's right."

"You have to do *something*, Tennessee. You can't give over to defeat. You just can't abandon the Vietnamese."

"Baby, what we're doing ain't doing much good."

7

Once the Benefit Committee had been established, Tom Seligson and I took the subway each day to our two-room office at Coalition headquarters and grappled with all the little problems that confront the dedicated revolutionary in organizational work within the movement: trying to free our telephones from the hippie drifters with the green fatigue backpacks who wandered in by the score and sat on my desk making long-distance phone calls to buddies on the Coast . . . to clear workrooms to do mailings and try to find the stamps we had purchased that morning that had disappeared into some brother's or sister's pocket during the intervening minutes it took me to take my coat off and get coffee . . . to clear rooms occupied by movement sisters holding sensitivity sessions, female members of our paid staff blowing the time holding kaffeeklatsches to bitch about the male chauvinism endemic to the most timid and self-effacing of their male coworkers . . . maneuvering my way through the workers of the Berrigan Defense Committee, who each day held interminable consciousness-raising sessions in the main room chaired by a priest . . . fighting with gay libbers over the use of our typewriters . . . arguing with black activists from Philadelphia and Boston who appeared en masse around noon to confront me with the question of whether this whitey honk-honk pig owed them lunch as reparations for his white skin privilege. One morning I found a hippie

the
gathering
of the
tribe

hitchhiker from somewhere west asleep in our broom closet. We were not running an office. We were running an outpatient clinic, a loony bin, Gawd! a banana farm for spaced-out neurotic hippie-Yippie sickos who would no more lick a stamp for the movement than they would take a subway when they could rip cab fare off some radical patsy.

And who were these whackos crowding our offices, these proud members of our class base, of the *lumpenproletariat*, tell me, who were these young, curiously affluent unemployed who whiled away the day smoking grass and drinking Boone's Farm apple wine and playing their goddamn FM radios at full power as I tried to wheedle agents on the Coast into giving us free acts and beg, borrow, or steal necessary funds from Manhattan fat cats so that we could in some way extend the effective life of the antiwar movement? By and large they were members of what was called the May Day Collective, the "youth wing" of the Peoples Coalition, if you can consider, that is, Stu Alpert's beer belly and gray hair as signs of youth. And it was they who fought us every inch of the way on every decision. And it was some of them who would, in the end, rip us off, their "comrades."

Let me briefly give you some example of the profound ideological differences between the May Day crowd, especially its women's caucus, and the rest of us.

We decided to invite Don McLean to sing at the benefit. The women's caucus vetoed him on the grounds that his hit song, "American Pie," was sexist.

"Sexist! Are you out of your goddamned minds!" I was outraged. He was a *star*. He would sell seats. He was *needed*.

"It's sexist! It's about beauty queens. It objectifies women. It is objectively chauvinist and counterrevolutionary!" They had a way with words, these women.

"You know something, should I tell you something . . . you . . . I'm so completely at a loss with you people, at your pigheadedness, your sheer, bigoted, unrelenting *stupidity*. 'American Pie' is about *us*. About the sixties. About it all being over."

"Sexist!"

" 'Bye, bye Miss American Pie, Drove my chevy to the levee but the levee was dry and them good ole-boys—"

"Chauvinist!"

"—'were drinkin' whisky and rye, singing this will be the day that I die . . .' "

"Shut up! You pig!"

" *'The day the music died.'* That's *us.*"

I lost.

They bitched that Gloria Steinem, who was one of the most helpful friends the Coalition had, was an "opportunist glamour pig." Charming. That she was cashing in on "their" women's revolution.

The women prevented the showing of a powerful antiwar short, *The Star-Spangled Banner,* because it contained a shot of an exposed female breast. There was a totally naked man in it, but the breast rattled them. Sexist, you understand. I even had Dave Dellinger come over to the office on that one, to attempt to convince the women that two-and-a-half-second breast shots were not always necessarily sexist. We lost.

The May Day Collective forced a ban on the use of union members as marshals in the cathedral because they were "too bourgeois and culturally unliberated." Instead, they forced on us a security contingent composed of their own members and, with the support of Rennie Davis, gave us as head of security a former member of Army intelligence (talk about a contradiction in terms).

Blood, Sweat and Tears, the rock group, was attacked for being State Department "running dogs." They had once made a tour of Eastern Europe under American government sponsorship. "Think of the *ends,*" I kept shouting. "Think of the *goals.* We want money, don't you understand? Publicity. We have five thousand goddamn empty seats!" And I always thought Marxists believed the ends justified the means.

The biggest fight, and the one in which we refused to give ground and in which Dellinger and every person in a leadership position supported us, was over whether Norman Mailer would be invited on the Committee and asked to speak and present his play *D.J.* (based on *Why Are We in Vietnam?*) at the cathedral. I had already gone ahead and invited him, and I was so convinced of the necessity of his appearance that I threatened to quit if he were thrown off. If he had no place in the movement, then neither did I. Poor Mailer, he wasn't distinguished by the quality of his enemies. Every day at the mention of his name—*whammo!* Sexist male chauvinist pig right-wing opportunist objectively contrary to Marxist-Leninist-Maoist liberation counterrevolutionary cake-eater rip-off artist decadent bourgeois culture-vulture running dog. . . .

Thus, organizationally, every day Seligson and I argued and fought and finally tried to ignore these revolutionaries whose idea of a political action was to rip off a new rock LP at Korvette's. And, in the end, we lost, as did the movement. You see, they could not distinguish enemies from friends. They were democratic in that, and while I was all for democracy, it was impossible to organize anything if the people you worked with continually disrupted what you were doing. It made no sense to me. I kept thinking, *This* is the best we have? *This* is our leadership cadre?

In three months working on the benefit, all my time devoted to its organization, it became clearer to me that our actions on the left no longer fit the times, that our reflexive responses to historic events had become false. We had failed in imagination if not in resolve. The failure of the Remember the War Benefit was due partly to my own incompetence and inexperience but also to a general misunderstanding of the age. We were trapped in the sixties, actors confusing lines. Our gestures had become melodramatic and too large, the sensibility and rhetoric untrue. We kept on like a handful of dizzy officers on a plain with no army left to lead, only we would not admit it to ourselves. No one looked over his shoulder to see that no one was following behind.

The benefit then, in an odd way, became the last hurrah for that era, at least for me. For gathered there that night, playing one more rerun of the same show we had carried on the road across the country since Port Huron, were many of the commanding figures of that era: Mailer, Dellinger, Williams, Rubin, on and on. It was a final gathering of the tribe. For something had changed in American history, had changed the emotional space in which we acted, and people were turning away from collective consciousness and involvement, from risk. And regardless of how often, due to dramatic event, they again would take to the streets, I became convinced that the era we represented, in which we made our politics, was over.

8

I spent the morning of the benefit at the Coalition office. Tom Seligson was at the cathedral trying to oversee the completion of the construction of the stage in front of the high altar, a massive platform elevated sixteen feet above the Cathedral floor for which we were paying the outrageous rent of $10,000 from William J. Hanley and Sons. Joshua Light never showed to create the light show. Electrical cables were late in being installed. The usual last-minute problems.

I called Dave Dellinger around noon, because I was worried about two developments. First, we had received two calls, one from Philadelphia, the other from Washington, warning us that several women's cadres were coming up to Manhattan in order to trash Mailer when he rose to speak. We had to tighten his security. I thought then that I should have accepted Mailer's suggestion, scotched his speech and the play, and had a boxing ring constructed in front of the altar and fought him there. He said we should bill it as the Fight of the Century, between the Left-Conservative (Mailer) and the Left-Radical (me). The trouble was, I don't know how to box.

It is curious, but from the very beginning I had a sense of dread concerning Mailer's appearance. I could see him shot down, see him climbing the platform and a rifle shot shattering his brain . . . and I was of two minds about that eventuality. I was fond of Mailer, so I did not want it

save
the
last dance
for me

to happen, and yet I knew there was something appropriate about such an occurrence. I sensed he wanted it. Perhaps I was simply projecting my own neurosis, because I know that when I was told by a palmist that I would die violently before the age of sixty I found the prediction to my liking.

I suggested to Dellinger that we ask William Douthard, a very strong man who was a Coalition coordinator and who could be trusted absolutely, to handle Tennessee's and Mailer's personal security. Dellinger agreed. I called Mailer and told him what I had learned. It did not seem to bother him in the slightest. And that bothered me.

I told Dave about my misgivings about our security in general. I had learned the night before that some of the members of our security force had met over dinner and discussed how to rip off the benefit. They had decided to steal the collection and also, because these were members of the streets-belong-to-the-people people, they would neglect to guard the doors, since music also belonged to the people. In principle I could agree, but the sixty-thousand-dollar debt moderated my enthusiasm for putting such a belief into practice. In a word, they planned to screw the antiwar movement; anyone would be allowed inside the cathedral whether he purchased a ticket or not. (The tickets were priced from $3.50 to $100.)

Dellinger said he would speak to the security people. He was sure I was alarmed over idle talk.

That afternoon it began to rain. I went to my apartment, where a film crew arrived, under the direction of Tom Hedley. They were making a documentary of the benefit for the CBC–BBC. I was filmed shaving, talking on the phone, dressing . . . filmed in the taxi going to the Plaza to pick up Ruth Ford and Tennessee Williams.

I arrived at the hotel late. Ruth and Tennessee and his sister Rose were waiting. Tennessee was dressed in a gray Confederate uniform. He was high and happy. His agent, Billy Barnes, was with him. I sensed some nervousness. While the crew filmed us, I briefed Tennessee on the latest statistics from the war: the dead and wounded, the bomb tonnage, troop numbers, the count of the antiwar Americans still in jails, etc.

"Hmmm. . . ." He was writing the statistics down on note-paper as I gave them to him. "Am I the only one who's going to give statistics? Because I don't want somebody else to, uh, you know . . . steal it! Ha! Ha! Now let's get this reasonably accurate, if we can, approximate at any rate."

"They're correct," I said. "I got them from Dave."

"Fifty-four thousand American death toll?"

"Right."

"North and South Vietnam and Cambodia and Laos . . . over a million death toll, mostly noncombatant. Nearly four hundred thousand wounded American boys." He took off his glasses, sighing.

"Now I will tell you, Tenn. There're going to be boys from various veterans' hospitals brought there tonight. We just raised the money to bring them there tonight. They'll be near the stage. We want the television cameras to catch them."

"Hmmm . . ." He put his glasses back on. He was suddenly terribly serious, writing. "Paraplegics and amputees . . . double and triple and quadruple, no, they can't be quadruple amputees. Two million wounded Asians? *Two million?* And when they say wounded you don't know how badly wounded they really are. Some of them would prefer to be dead, I should think. And when does it stop, Dotson? By whose secret schedule does this mass slaughter end, this shame-fully criminal war stop?"

I sat back. The cameras filmed him. The room was very silent. All of a sudden Tennessee had begun his speech, or at least the expression of his feelings on the war.

He continued: "Will it only be when another war begins and when it's begun? What does the military-industrial system depend upon? Where is Kilroy's way out? And yours and ours?"

Tennessee began writing again, mumbling to himself.

"Young Americans . . . and American dissidents . . . and American war protesters, eh? In prison on war-related offenses, baby?"

I said: "And that means resisting the draft, refusing to register, arrested for conspiracy to duck the draft, and that's why Jann Eller is standing trial, for assaulting an officer and conspiracy to commit riot, conspiracy to oppose the draft." Tennessee did not catch the name. "Eller—remember, Tenn? The blond kid?" He nodded. "Well, you know what's happening to him?"

"Yeah. He's facing a possible life sentence."

"And for what!" Now I was excited. "For *what*? He did nothing. Did I tell you that, Billy? About Jann?" I turned to Tennessee's agent. "He's a kid who was arrested, he sold the *Berkeley Barb*, at Merritt College, which is where Huey Newton and Bobby Seale went. He was arrested at the bus stop carrying his papers under his arm with half a brick in his pocket, which he used to hold down the papers in the wind. And he was arrested for assault on a police officer with a deadly weapon, uh, possession of a deadly weapon, and in California you get what is known as an indeterminate sentence, two years to life, which is what George Jackson went in for. *He* stole seventy dollars, and he spent seven years until they finally murdered him in the prison yard."

Tennessee writing, "Jann *Eller* is the name of this . . . how do you spell it?"

"E-l-l-e-r."

"I remember him quite well." Tennessee smiled. "We got him out of jail, didn't we? Temporarily." Tennessee had sent him bail money.

"Bail, right."

"And what was he charged with?"

"Possession of a deadly weapon." We were back on the same routine again.

"Possession of a deadly weapon?" Puzzled.

"A half brick." I was getting exasperated.

"What was the deadly weapon?" He did not understand.

"*The half brick he had in his pocket.* To hold down the papers."

"Yes," Ruth said, "they can fall out of a building at any moment." She and I laughed. Tennessee did not.

"There must be something else besides that, isn't there?" It made no sense whatsoever to him, jailed for half a brick, school papers, deadly weapons . . .

I explained it again, at great length. Tennessee finally got the confusion straightened out and started scribbling fast. "Waited a year . . . arrested at a bus stop . . . for carrying half a brick."

"For carrying half a brick *in his pocket, concealing,* concealing a deadly weapon was the charge. And the jury, where he was going to trial the jury is all, you know, redneck whites. He's not charged, I mean *tried* by his *peers,* you know, he's tried by the people who hate what he stands for and his long hair." I knew he was going to speak at the benefit about Jann. I wanted to make sure *he* was sure he understood the details.

Tennessee: "Then you would say it was a . . . uh, statutory injustice? In Reagan country. . . ."

"Right! And part of what we are doing tonight is trying to raise money for his defense."

Writing it down. "We're trying to raise money to defend young Americans like him . . . for his defense . . ."

Finally we left. We were forty minutes late.

In the taxi I asked Ruth Ford to stay with Tennessee. He had never spoken at a political rally before. I must say something about Ruth Ford. It was she who gave us the essential advice and aid we needed, not in terms of hard politics but in terms of raising money and support. And what she gave of even greater value was enormous tolerance—mine had run out—and style to what we attempted to do. Dellinger was correct when he said that she was one of the great dividends the peace movement earned through the benefit.

We arrived about six-thirty, an hour before the benefit itself was to begin in the cathedral, but an hour after the press reception had started. We went immediately to the Synod House, a small building directly across from the cathedral, where the Committee was giving the press party. Tennessee, who had no great love for Norman Mailer, said he would only stand by him a minute, just so the photographers could do their stuff, and that was all. He was worried Mailer would use dirty language and embarrass the movement. "If he uses a dirty word I'm going to punch him in the nose! The movement can't afford that kind of publicity, not now, not in the church!"

There was a large press contingent, several hundred from the United States and Europe, and most of the members of the Committee were there, as were the performers: the Chamber Brothers, Charles Mingus, Edgar Winter and White Trash, Tuli Kupferberg, Phil Ochs. Richard Avedon had set up a studio area and was hauling various celebrities before his camera. He grabbed Tennessee and Ruth immediately.

As soon as I walked in, Tom Seligson drew me aside.

"It's falling apart!"

"What is?"

"The whole thing! People are being admitted without tickets! There're no security people in the church. They're all here. We're going *bankrupt!*" And sure enough, there, with a score of other marshals, was our chief of security drinking a highball. He raised his glass, grinning.

About five thousand people attended the benefit concert. People with fifty-dollar tickets sat beside people with none. Welfare Rights Mothers carried placards, as did a group of squatters feuding with the Episcopal Church over church-owned apartments; a group of crazies with NLF flags stood like clowns in front of the enormous stage and waved them in front of the network television crews; gay lib activists passed out leaflets; and a group of Young Lords stood on the far side of the stage staring defiantly out at the crowd, the buttons on their jackets catching the lights.

Bishop Moore, a tall, handsome, gaunt man, opened the

program by welcoming us, as representatives of the entire peace movement, to his church. He was followed by a tape recording made by a Vietnamese soldier-poet which had been smuggled to us the day before via Eastern Europe. It was especially recorded for the evening. Charles Mingus played, followed by Edgar Winter and White Trash. Then Ruth Ford, Tennessee Williams, and I climbed onto the stage. We stood while Dave Dellinger spoke of the war and of the young people across this country in prison for draft resistance and antiwar activities for whom the collection was being taken. Dellinger knew by that point, as did I, that the gate had been lost. And there we stood, totally helpless, watching some of our security marshals collecting thousands of dollars. (The take was estimated later to have been in excess of five thousand dollars and, instead of bringing the collection to the stage where Dellinger was to receive it, they were strolling with it out the great doors of the cathedral into the night.)

Ruth introduced Tennessee. He walked to the microphone. The cathedral was dark except for the spotlight focused on him. He seemed terribly small and vulnerable.

Tennessee spoke about the heavy responsibility of all Americans for war in Vietnam. He spoke of Jann Eller and others who resisted. "There is no business as usual with this evil, immoral war. We must not stop the protests until it is ended. Until all the peacemakers are free and the war is over. Now I am too old to march anymore"—the audience yelled No! No!, and Tennessee raised his hand to silence them—"but I will march on paper!"

On the way off the platform I introduced Tennessee to Gloria Steinem, who had preceded Dellinger and Ossie Davis in speaking. He did not know who she was, although he was impressed by her speech. "She is a very influential feminist writer," I said. "She's been in the movement a long time."

He looked at her, smiling. "My, and so young!"

Mailer followed Tennessee. He stood on stage with his hands thrust in his pockets, jacketless, his legs spread. There was great tension as he spoke, and he was heckled and booed at points. "Now we have to face into the future," he concluded, "which is curious, because a mood of revolution has come upon the young in America, and when that war in Vietnam is over, you have to ask yourself what you will do next, what are your values going to be, what are your desires going to be when there will no longer be a war in Vietnam to boo. And I tell you it is a good reason to pause and reflect and try to say to yourself what indeed is that revolutionary future going to bring? . . . The more we go in for self-righteousness and piety beyond this point, the more we are in danger of becoming left-wing totalitarians. That is the danger when we all of us get together."

There was some light applause and some heckling. Mailer then turned and introduced his cast: Beverly Bentley, Rip Torn, and Paul Gilford. He left the stage.

The play lasted about forty-five minutes. Somewhere in the middle of it Tennessee got up and walked off, offended by the language. Perhaps a third or more of the audience left before Mailer's play was completed. Arguments broke out backstage. As the extent of our financial loss began to be recognized, various creditors started yelling at Dellinger, Seligson, and myself, demanding immediate payment. Finally, Seligson and I sat a moment in the choir loft behind the stage listening to Mailer's words read by Rip Torn. Seligson started shaking, desperately trying to hold back tears. "The bastards! The bastards! They've robbed the movement, their friends. Three months' work shot to hell by those lousy sons of bitches. I never trusted them, even when Rennie said they were okay, I never trusted those . . ."

I waited until the end of Mailer's play. And then I slipped out through a side entrance, avoiding the press and creditors, and headed for Joe Allen's bar and got drunk. It was over.

A week later an accounting was made. We lost more than nine thousand dollars on the evening. The American press coverage was light, although the event received heavy play in Europe, primarily due to the presence of Mailer and Williams. There was some damage to the cathedral. A youth hurt his back falling from the stage. Another broke a leg. I did not break a leg, but the experience broke something inside me beyond repair. And the Peoples Coalition? It was in worse shape than before the benefit. As was Bishop Moore, who suddenly found himself under fierce attack for allowing us to use the cathedral.

We held two very unpleasant meetings with the security people we knew had stolen the money. Dave Dellinger chaired the meetings, which were held at Norma Becker's house. The thieves denied the theft to the end, although they returned two hundred and fifty dollars of the monies taken. Dellinger finally compiled a list of those involved in the theft. He was deeply saddened by the betrayal. But what could we do? To press it legally would mean making public the names of those responsible for the act. And because of the association of many of them with respected movement organizations, such a public legal action would do the movement more damage than the loss of funds. Anyway, we did not believe in the police. The crooks had us by the short hairs, and they knew it.

When I told Tennessee about the theft, and about my despondency over it, my sense of having been betrayed, he shook his head and said, "Well, I hope they spent it on something nice." What else was there to say? The benefit was a bust.

Gus Hall was not at the benefit, although the party was represented in the Peoples Coalition. The party worked in the Coalition because it believed in the concept of the Popular Front and collective action tied to specific issues. The party sought hegemony over the left, and what excited its rancor was the continuing refusal of the New Left and the antiwar movement to bend to the party's line. The party's youth arm, the Young Workers Liberation League, was very small and hopelessly ineffective. It could not compete politically or emotionally with the appeal of the highly unstructured New Left. And so the party dreamt of the collapse of the New Left, and it was in the habit of announcing with distressing regularity that collapse, the wish being father to the thought.

Indeed, later that winter, Gus Hall got into his old Plymouth and drove from his home in Yonkers to New York, where he addressed a Communist party congress and announced, to his enthusiastic comrades, the death (again) of the New Left.

He was wrong. The New Left had not died. However, Hall's announcement was relevant to me and to what I had lived through. Something had died in me, whose passing rendered me embittered and adrift. Bereaved. Something of the hope that had sustained me for a decade and in which I no longer believed. Life had been emptied, and there was nothing around I could grab to fill it up.

part two

ALTER-
NATIVES

9

There are stages in life that are as predictable and immutable as the seasons, certain points in time where a personal summing-up occurs naturally, a period of adjustment, to use Williams's phrase, where detachment from one's own life happens dramatically and you sense that a plateau has been reached: what is past is over, and disengagement from it has commenced. At these times, when your grip on life fails, if your friends or family are not supportive or if booze or drugs or sexual confusion or public defeat intrude massively in your life, then panic sets in. You are open to anything.

The end of adolescence and the beginning of middle age are two such points of crisis. Another one, the most unacknowledged, is when one nears and passes the age of thirty, for it is then that you realize that you are now what you will be until you die. And if you do not like yourself, what then?

That was where I was situated, in the beginning of 1972, seven months from my thirtieth birthday, like a joy-boy gone impotent, trucking into panic. My response? Increased dependency on old friends—liquor and Demerol and Ritalin—to fight new ones—insomnia and fear. I was conscious of the end of many things important to me, or their distancing themselves away from me, and I was at a loss to know what to do.

If I alone had begun to break it would not have mat-

trucking
into
panic

tered much, but the hell of it was that I saw others of my generation experiencing the same difficulties in identity and sex and work, the same recourse to drugs, as if blind stupor were an answer to fear and purposelessness. I am generalizing. Suffice it to say that a significant number of friends with whom I started out in the sixties and with whom I shared similar experience and politics began to fall apart in the first years of the seventies, and what is of some interest is that they were better and stronger than I, brighter and more sensitive, and yet they did not make it through. Since I cannot speak for them, I have to tell you how it was for me, something of the alternatives that tempted me, violence and drugs, and of the hard attempt to find a role, a function, to replace activism when it no longer worked for me.

The Remember the War Benefit was an unimportant event in terms of its public impact. That is why it was a failure. Its importance to me was that it forced me to contend with a change in my experience in America, something others in the movement also had to contend with. I understood that the movement in which I was active was changing form and that to continue my usual participation in it was to be false to it and to myself. It was not that my politics had changed; rather, the narrow corridor of history in which the movement played had bent away from me, leaving my sensibility inadequate to it, my responses untrue. Again, something had shifted in history, clearly by 1969, and to continue acting as I had was foolish. Dream stuff. It was to act totally without effect, and if in part manhood meant effectiveness, then to remain a street activist when collective activism was increasingly seen as counterproductive and ineffective was to act against my manhood.

The question became: What do I do now with my life?

As I have said, I believed that the era of mass protest was over, an insight that neatly coincided with my feeling that my youth was over. It was not that the movement could not, with extraordinary effort or with the luck presented to it by the mistakes of its enemies, entice hundreds of thousands of people into the streets. No, it was the notion that such a feat meant very little. It was inappropriate because power, the ability to intimidate your enemy, no longer resided in mass protest. Anyway, I was not certain I was interested in that kind of power anymore.

Objectively the left always sought power in the name of others, since its leadership was often recruited from groups more educated and privileged than those it worked to serve. It struggled on behalf of the powerless and unprivileged, the poor and oppressed. But to struggle for power in that way was to live as surrogate, abstractly and collectively, and it required great sacrifice from you, not so much in terms of economic loss or living conditions, but in more subtle and damaging ways. It required that you choose against your past, the people and class from which you came, and thus against something that was indelibly part of your being. You had to construct a fiction about those people to insert in the vacuum that was your past, because to love your past was to know disloyalty to what you had chosen to become; it was to love the values and privilege you now opposed.

So much of the sorrow shown as rage on the left by the young was a result of this constant imperative to despise your roots. During the Columbia Liberation of 1968, every thread of worker's denim, every repressed impulse to privacy and sexual pairing, the openness to arrest and expulsion, all the puritanical denial of liquor and good food and, at the end, even grass, spoke of the struggle to rebuke what was seen of the enemy inside the young radical's skin. And it was all unnecessary, all a waste. Lenin lived like a petit bourgeois in Swiss exile while we trudged through the halls of Mathematics looking for the revolution. So much of it seems to me now to have been naïve (we wanted so badly not to repeat the mistakes of our fathers, not to sell out to anything) and, in a manner I am only now beginning to understand, mutilating. To reject overnight conventions and feelings which were your nature, to roughen up, to adopt a role, try so hard to learn it, be what your parents warned you against . . . the bill for it is coming due.

I loved the left. I love it now. But it is a jealous thing. The sons of the middle and privileged classes occupied a nether world between all classes and established realities, a band of renegades filled with self-doubt and compensatory rage and that moral certitude that passes at thirty. A nether world because you cannot go back to what you have come to hate, and yet you know you will never finally belong to what you have opted to serve. Nothing you could do, once commitment against the past was made, allowed more than conditional entry to the world abandoned or the new, poorer one chosen. I do not believe that people who are poor all their lives ever trust the sons of privilege come to serve them. Nor should they. That too, the sensing of distrust, was part of what one paid, all of it extracted in the coin of guilt over what one could not help, one's birth and education and manners, and in estrangement from what one desperately wanted to join and which one worked to serve: the community of victims. The New Left was populated by ghosts. And yet if you were young and feeling and decent in the sixties, I think it was the only place to be. It was the best.

Sacrifice, then, was made for the sake of power. Our movement, because it existed noninstitutionally, because it was largely self-created and ad hoc and had no roots in official public mythology and tradition, because its nature was emotive and intuitive and antirational and anarchistic, was condemned to continually reinvent itself, to redefine its aims. Its ambitions remained constant (the will to power, like a sexual drive, is constant in its passion), while its immediate objectives shifted continually. It had to be reinvented every morning. Someone was always coming along with a new line or cause or political fashion, and like a meth spike shoved in an adolescent arm, these new intrusions of concern and ideology acted on the movement the way speed does on the body. They gave a temporary rush, an energy high, and ended leaving the subject more debilitated and divided and fatigued and disoriented than before. It produced instability, if that word can be politically defined as the incapacity to establish lasting priorities. One was continually embracing and then abandoning modes of belief in light of new evidence or new demands or new situations resulting from a change in consciousness on the part of one radical constituency or another. One was continually out of step.

Mass protest was over because it did not work. It had lost its power. Much like a veteran junkie's tolerance for smack, the public's tolerance for street disruption had reached the point of disgruntled stupor. Apathy was the order, and massive protests intimidated no one. In that situation, by their very character, massive, collective, quasilegal actions could not address themselves to the actual sources of power, which were not to be found on the university campuses or in the streets. So I began to feel that it was incumbent on radicals to pursue more personal, and thus, in this new period, more effective responses to political actuality than those offered within wide collective action. I was no longer able to handle truth collectively. I could not locate it there. More and more I distrusted any reality outside my immediate senses. Everything else was beyond my reach.

What was the alternative, then, if mass street action was increasingly ineffective?

I still believed in the efficacy of violence. I responded to it positively on many levels, esthetically, sexually. I even discovered myself wishing to die violently, shot, say, coming out of my apartment building in the afternoon as I stopped in the doorway to open an umbrella because it was raining; seeing assassination as the ultimate flattery, a deadly kiss.

Here I want to discuss something of the political arguments in favor of violence, arguments current at the time which intrigued me, in order to explain why I didn't take that alternative, even though it was one I could see as large and productive enough to spend my life for.

Mass organizing and street action, married as they were in the United States to pacifist, reformist, nonrevolutionary movements, had little to do with revolutionary violence. If violence was to be successful in the United States (successful in that it hastened the overthrow of the capitalist state), it had to be undertaken by small, tightly disciplined, conspiratorial groups, *affinities*, underground, paramilitary, outside the law. That was the only form of public protest (in the sense that blowing up a bank for political reasons is public protest) that was still capable of intimidating the state, and that was a vital consideration to me, because I had lost all faith in liberal, corporate democracy, in discourse, reason, and compromise as tools of political reform within the given electoral system. Violence-as-intimidation and as propaganda therefore became the only revolutionary tool available, or at least of sufficient appeal to me. Considering the current situation on the left, it was the most practicable, being the most economic, entailing the expenditure of very little resource. It could be accomplished dramatically by very small numbers of people. Its effect was enormous, cumulative, and highly subversive—subversive of corporate, democratic institutions in that it furthered paranoia and distrust and reactive repression. The government always overreacted to left-wing violence, to the terrorist's advantage.

The first times I saw friends beaten by the police or arrested, and the first times people I knew died or were imprisoned, the first times, that is, I witnessed violence against my friends, I responded with outrage and desire for revenge. That was all muted now, and I began to understand violence not so much in terms of its capacity to satisfy some psychological need in me (revenge, for instance) but in terms of its political utility. It came to possess for me deeply human and life-giving qualities. That seems an apparent contradiction, but it is not.

In a highly technological, postindustrial system, one extremely vulnerable to economic disruption, radical violence was one of the few means of preserving something precious in human life. Revolutionary, anarchistic, even nihilistic violence (I am thinking in terms of violence against property, not persons) was objectively irrational—in the immediate, objective situation it was doomed to failure—and yet it was necessary and valuable *because* it was irrational. In American society, reason and technology had become the handmaidens of established power. It was the technocrat, the superclerk, with his rationalist, amoral, technical systemology, who controlled the rest of us. What was Vietnam if not technology detached from soul, murder devoid of passion? In such a controlled and technical world, revolutionary violence acquired positive moral value because it was objectively an (irrational) attack on rational systems that were dehumanizing. Compared with the deadly sterility of established order and its *im*personal—therefore dehumanizing—violence, revolutionary violence was lush with humanity, moral and life-enhancing.

The revolutionary act of violence was the individual declaring his existence and worth to a system that had reduced him to commodity.

Thus, such violence, because it was disruptive and antimanipulative, was a remedy for alienation, much as the acceptance of death was a remedy for fear. And if violence were wedded to beauty, a romantic, such as myself, was helpless before it. One of the terrible aspects of modern, postindustrial alienation was the blunting and fragmentation of the personality, the assault on manhood. Revolutionary violence for a moment allowed the integration of the personality, the man and the act became inseparable, and provided not only the sense of doing justice (because one was effectively, even in a small way, acting against a political-economic arrangement that was killing) but equality as well. For a moment, like warriors facing off in battle, one stood as equal with an enemy.

Let me try to put this into focus: conspiratorial violence was possible with very limited resources. It was an adequate response to technology since modern technology was excessively vulnerable to primitive weapons. A handmade bomb, even water, can destroy a computer system; helicopters, like men, are vulnerable to rifle shot. However, to be a revolutionary engaged in violence required the abandonment of one human quality to assert another. One had to abstract life from its particular context and assert that abstract Life could be salvaged only by wasting individual lives. A revolutionary had to disengage himself sufficiently from personal feeling to be able to view his enemies as abstractions, not people, as classes rather than as individuals. The enemy had to be drained of individual substance so that violence could be done to him; he had to be seen as part of the gang in the dock at Nuremberg awaiting execution, as outside human limits. My failing, and I saw it as such, was that I could not act on the basis of abstractions, not violently anyway. I kept seeing Nixon, for example, not as a mass murderer (which he objectively was) but as a pathetic individual, however dangerous, worthy of pity. I could see myself in him, in them all. If you are tempted to engage in revolutionary violence, it is very stupid to pity your enemy.

Illustration: Late in 1970, in New York, on a rainy, windy, miserable day, I participated in a demonstration against the war. The event was sponsored by the Fifth Avenue Parade Committee. It attracted several thousand protesters, an astonishing number of them of high-school age or younger. I saw barely a handful of middle-aged demonstrators, those who used to provide most of the cash and about one third of the movement's troops.

I walked along with the Westchester contingent until the march ended in the park. Hank was nominal leader of the group, I suppose by virtue of the fact that he hoisted the largest placard: BRING THE WAR HOME! After the demonstration I took Hank up to Columbia University, where I had gone to school for four years. We walked around the campus and I pointed out various landmarks: the Mathematics Building, the sundial, Hamilton Hall, the window of the president's office, all of which had figured in the Columbia Liberation protests of 1968, in which I had been active. As we strolled on campus I boasted away, feeling heroic in retrospect, like a Bolivian exile escaped to blather away about the historic days with Che.

"Why did you give up?" Hank asked as we crossed Broadway and went inside the West End bar. "How come you lost the liberation?"

A good question, yet considering the source, considering the fact that he had not been there at the time, I thought he was in no position to criticize us. My age showing, defensively; he was sixteen.

"There were the cop busts, you know. Awful things. And then a division in our camp. We were outnumbered."

"Why didn't you blow up some buildings or take more hostages? Why didn't you do something effective?"

"I'm not at Columbia anymore," I replied, by way of a dodge. "What we should do," I said, "is to organize the poor, the young workers, as in France, the armed forces. Win the generation. Christ, when the army's morale is destroyed, discipline wrecked, when the soldier wins his freedom and doesn't have to fight wars he hates, then, baby, the ball game's over for the capitalist." So simple.

Then Hank said, and this is where I knew I was dated, losing touch, knew the game had gone far beyond me, my courage inadequate to the plays, "I think we ought to assassinate Mayor Lindsay."

"Why?" I found the idea mad. He was sixteen, after all, and while he affected, as did most kids, working-class dress, and had been active on the left for over a year, taking two weeks off from high school to participate in the troubles at San Francisco State, still he remained a boy from a wealthy family, a kid jetting to revolution. *Kill* the *Mayor*?

He looked at me like *I* was nuts. "Why? Because every goddamn left-lib will *ask* why, *that's* why! To most Americans it makes no sense."

"It makes none to me." I laughed, not wanting to take him seriously.

"Listen, it'll polarize the country, scare the pigs pissless. . . ."

"It'll produce repression if the government can hang it on us. You have to think of your brothers, its effect on them." In that and similar situations, where I was being outmaneuvered to my left, I adopted, I suppose defensively, a moderate, *reasonable* line. Odd. Young kids talking of murder always scared me as if there were something obscene to it, to play with the risks of death when life was untasted. That, as I have been told, was "age chauvinism" on my part, for I felt no similar disquiet when people my own age speculated on violence. It was inappropriate, *calculated* violence, in the very young, which was indecent.

He was unperturbed. "Sure. But repression's coming anyway. It's halfway here already. They'll get all of us, one by one. Hell, let's bring the fascism out in the open. Let's at least make the country honest. They hate us and the blacks and the young workers, students, so give them the excuse to show their hand. . . ." On and on, listing the reasons for murder.

"But he's a *decent* man," I said, defending Lindsay, his decency being about the only positive thing I could think of going for him. "Maybe incompetent, but certainly decent."

"Decent? He's the best, the very best the system's produced. Don't you understand? That's *why* we should assassinate him, because he *is* the best. Killing him, that'll keep the best away. If you can justify killing Lindsay, if you can politically justify that, then you can justify killing anyone." It was like something out of a Russian novel, his reasoning. It was unreal to me then, what he was saying, the enthusiasm and conviction with which he advanced his argument.

"If you've got to thrill kill, why not shoot Nixon or General Westmoreland? Why pick on poor Lindsay? What the hell's he done to deserve that?" I was getting angry. The boy *believed* what he said.

"Because, Dotson." Infinite patience in his voice. "Those men are not dangerous, not in the long run. They play their roles too well. They're *obviously* the enemy, fascists, but Lindsay, the Lindsays are front men who give people false hope in the system. They think, if Big John's on the job, if the system produces him, then maybe we should give the system time to reform. Well, there ain't any hope, and Big John shields the pigs, makes people think revolution isn't needed. Assassinating him, wow! Like, that would break the goddamn rules, that would break them for good."

"You have to make a better case than that." Tired, thinking about a kid I talked through the night with in Boston who was planning to blow up City Hall, had the lousy blueprints and traffic patterns, knew the security system of the new building. His reasons were the same. Only he was fifteen. I felt overwhelming responsibility for all the kids.

"It's so *obvious*. Can't you see? Lindsay's complicit in the system. Like, he's part of it, man. Like, why should any politician, even if he isn't a phony, be immune to death when the Vietnamese aren't, the poor, the blacks, the draftees aren't? Why should only the system use violence and not those who oppose it? It's a class thing that kills, Lindsay's bourgeois class. . . ."

I agreed that the state should not be granted the monopoly on violence, and that people should not be free of the consequences of their acts. In attacking the Harvard School of International Affairs, for which Eric Mann was jailed, the Weatherman was trying to bring the war home, to bring to the academics who formulated imperialist policy the consequences of that policy, to remove their immunity from the results of their plotted violence against others. But I could not see killing Mayor Lindsay. Not because I valued the kid Hank more, nor thought that in the balance his life was more valuable than Lindsay's and therefore the bargain was a bad one; rather, it was because *indirect* complicity in murder was too indirect for me to make life and death judgments on anymore. I had not the heart for it.

Let me put it another way: I found great beauty in violence. I do not know if that was because we are primates who became hunters and consequently violence is intrinsic to our nature; or whether it was because violence is fundamentally sexual aggression. It is indisputable that until recently in the history of man violence by males against other males was the chief means of taking mates. Violence had great sexual value, women being, as it were, trophies awarded to the most competent in fighting. Therefore, the impulse always lies inside the male and is released, in however mutilated and attenuated a manner, in every sexual act. What I do know is that the possibility of it continually festered inside me, and that, for me, to act violently was to act naturally. It was fulfilling. What can I say? I concluded then that to try and impose political rationales on what was, for me, an instinctive and sexual response to realities that were, by and large, apolitical was, if not fraudulent, certainly unnecessary. I needed no political reasons. I had other reasons enough.

Nevertheless, I was convinced that the level of one's temptation to violence was directly related to one's sexual security. That was why violence was so common among young males and decreased as males aged. It was the young lions after all who instinctively sought to employ their one natural advantage against the older, dominant males: their greater capacity and skill at violence. Sons against fathers. Admitting that, it was an unhappy thing to confess that after so long a time I was still teased by the drama of violence, something more appropriate to adolescents, something that should have ended with growing up, left behind in the locker room after the senior prom.

And that is one of the reasons why, in early 1972, suddenly confronted with disillusionment over the movement and the need to redefine my role, I abandoned the idea of

direct involvement in conspiratorial violence. Five years before, under similar circumstances, I think I would have
enthusiastically engaged in that role. Now it was five years
too late. I was too old, too emptied of the necessary discipline, worn of courage. No matter how much ideologically I
could support cadres training for urban revolution in the
cities of America, I could not engage in it myself. And while
I despised the fact, I could not compel my imagination to be
younger than it was, nor force my body to take orders from
a mind dreaming of street fighting.

Back to the beginning. I believed the era of mass street
protest was finished. I saw an alternative in conspiratorial
violence; in fact, I saw it as the best recourse available to
the committed revolutionary. But I was not a revolutionary,
had not the heart or the courage for it. What was I to do?

The alternatives became more modest and more real. I
could continue public organizing, and I could write. Writing
seemed an alternative, something I could do well and, in a
small way, effectively. There was no other option fitted to
me. It is true, I think, that writers write because they cannot act.

I am going to tell you about my experience with a number
of people during this period—Tennessee Williams, Yevtushenko, Jann Eller and other youths—in order to explain
my movement from one role to another, how these people,
two writers and some young men trucking into total loss,
determined in large measure what I did.

I also want to tell you about panic, about breaking down.

Nineteen seventy-two was a major point in my life and in
the lives of many other Americans my age. In the first part
of this book I tried to sketch something of the history of my
involvement on the left and of the failure and disillusionment that brought me here. Now I want to tell you where
that disillusionment took me, and what it cost.

10

Tennessee Williams was leaving New York. He called me early one morning from the Plaza Hotel, his voice very hoarse and tired, and asked me to stop by for lunch that afternoon and then take him to the airport. "I'm going to sleep now, baby. Uh, some actor is coming to sit in the other room while I sleep. I don't want to be alone, baby, you know?"

Shortly after eleven I arrived at the hotel. Williams's door was answered by a handsome, dark-haired young man wearing a white bath towel. The actor.

"Hi!" he exclaimed. One word, and I knew I was dealing with a dumbo.

"How's Tennessee?" I asked, walking into the sitting room of the suite.

"Tennessee?" The kid went completely blank.

"The man in the other room."

He grinned. "Oh, him. He's sleeping. I looked in when I got here. He was sleeping."

I nodded. "Good. He had a bad night."

"Sure . . . listen, man, I need cab fare."

I looked the young man over: nineteen years old, I guessed, probably Italian. "Why don't you get dressed?" He was naked except for the bath towel.

The question caught him unprepared. He thought a moment. "I'm doing exercises." He began doing deep knee

shifting

bends, dropping his towel, grinning idiotically at me as he bobbed up and down.

"No, stop that! This isn't a gym, for Christ's sake! We've got to get out of here. Tennessee has to catch a plane for New Orleans."

The youth stood up, looking at me in a way that seemed smug, a bit sultry, a hint of the knowing false innocence of a Caravaggio, a Saint John the Baptist disrobed and inviting; he was tugging, not at all absentmindedly, on his foreskin with one hand as he stared at me. "I need cab fare." Insistent now.

"I'll give you twenty bucks, okay? Now get dressed." I wanted him out of the room fast, and I did not want him haggling with Tennessee in the bedroom over sitter's payment. I was irritated by him, by the kind of sexual teasing I had witnessed so many times in young men and which I found increasingly disagreeable. It was not homosexuality in the abstract which bothered me—I was morally indifferent to that. Rather, it was the exploitation the tease represented, the tawdriness and manipulation, the boring cocksureness. That I resented when applied to me, the attitude that everyone was makable. Everyone was there to be had.

"Twenty bucks?" He sounded disappointed. He was fishing for more.

"You *ate*, didn't you? I see dirty dishes all over the goddamn table. What'd you order, steak?"

"I had eggs. They were cold."

"Sorry. But at least you were fed."

"Him. . . ." He gestured with his thumb toward the bedroom, speaking in a whisper. "He's a singer on the television?" Sin-*ger*, as in Long *Gi*-land.

"Yeah, sure," I said and pulled twenty bucks out of my pocket and gave it to him. "You better get dressed." He stood his ground, tugging on his penis with his hand, his mouth slightly open and smiling. For a moment I hated him, my jaw tightening, hated the hustling bastards. And then it passed. I shrugged. They also have to live the life.

"Come on, kid. Please get dressed."

He gave one more pull on his member and then drew on his clothes.

After he left I went into the bedroom to check on Williams. He seemed very small and strangely delicate and young huddled under the covers. Sixty years old, yet to me he seemed half that age. I pulled a blanket off the empty twin bed and threw it over him. By the side of his bed was a pile of newly published university textbooks with student editions of his plays. The room was a mess of scattered towels and clothes and papers and bottles and dirty cups and records and review books and manuscript pages and un-opened mail.

I poured myself a vodka. I leaned against the wall between the two windows overlooking Central Park and watched the smoke from my cigarette curl in the hard winter sunlight. I could hear Williams's labored breathing. I felt great love for him. I thought of him as a kind of warrior in the dark heat of a long battle, and I was sentimental enough in the warmth of the room and alcohol to think that Williams did everyone, especially writers, great honor by his struggle and survival. And I envied him, not his fame and money, which held little interest for me, but his tenacious grip on truth, on the essentials of survival. While in many areas he was self-indulgent and undisciplined, in his writing he was sure and true. I knew that when he was young he had associated with socialist writers, and that he had come to playwriting almost by accident. But once come into it, into writing, he never let go. Nothing ever bent him away from his craft. While we shared so many concerns in common, Williams always found the means to express them in his work. And that I envied, that discipline and patience. There was no false labor to him.

Suddenly I felt the urge to fight on his behalf, and if the youth (actor) had been there, I think I might have tried to slug him out. Although I could not consciously comprehend where the nexus between my love for Williams and my contempt for the youth joined, somewhere they surely did. For I was, in a way I either did not know or would not admit to myself, threatened in a manner reaching to my manhood by the youth's half-opened, smiling mouth. And my urge to defend Williams (who needed no defense) was born of a reality or fiction about myself, about my sexuality, which I could not then afford to abandon, something I had been defending in the streets every time I assumed the role of activist. Only the streets held no place for me anymore, they were emptied of allure.

Even now I am not sure of the final definition of that reality or fiction about myself. I know it was formed during my first years in New York when I lived for a time in the streets and hustled in the life. What I hustled with was a body and face and wits enough to know when to cover and when to protect, and what to sense about a man which made him tractable, what weaknesses were there to be laid hold of, what gave you the edge. I saw life as combat between unequal sides. The youth in Williams's room reminded me of something in myself I wanted to extinguish, which I had left behind, paid for and abandoned. I do not know how to articulate what that was except to say that if you are on the streets among the bleeding dirt, punk kids up for grabs, your obsession is for the means to take you from the streets, for freedom, before what is there kills you, before, that is, you surrender your will to drugs or parlor faggotry and go under. One of the aspects of growing up, if you were ever such a kid, is that you begin to *need* to look upon men you admire, as I looked upon Williams and Dellinger and even Mailer, as something of fathers to you at whatever remove. And the bleeding dirt, the punks, become yourself as son, and you want to relate to them in that way, as sons. And the politics of dissent become the politicization of combat between fathers and sons.

I was either more moralistic than I admitted or more jaded: sex devoid of feeling, and therefore responsibility, was a matter of barter for me, a form of exchange and therefore demeaning and, in what it carried to me of the memory of the street, threatening. What I hated in the kid, what I had contempt for, was that memory of myself before politics and before manhood: the street hustle. What was I, if not someone who had finally reached the other side of the street? The kid had nothing to exchange with me except intimacy with hunger, and I could not accept sex between men without exchange being involved—money, concern— of sufficient nonsexual value to justify the act, since pleasure itself was not enough, not when to fuck another man was to gamble with your manhood as surely as you wagered it every time you took to the streets in political confrontation. That too was a kind of lovemaking between men.

When Mailer had suggested that we construct a ring in the cathedral and have the Fight of the Century, I said I could not box, but that Tom Seligson could. "Why don't you fight Tommy?"

Mailer curled his lip. "He's got no *rep*."

Well, the kid had no rep, and if you were going to chance the conflict in your manhood by going up the dirt road with punks (however like yourself they might be), matters of sub-stance had to balance in the act.

I said that street politics was like lovemaking. And yet it was nobler, because great matters were at stake, how the community was to exist. If dissent was combat between fathers and sons (regardless of the sides they were on, whether opponents or allies, the conflict existed), then it was incestuous and therefore vastly dangerous, because ranks of identity were bet on the outcome of the game. What the kid dragged into the room, what his manner and face spoke, was the hustle. *I was beyond that.* He had to be a son —I was in search of them—or nothing.

After helping Tennessee pack, the two of us (I very tall, Tennessee very short) went to the bar downstairs for lunch. I had to borrow a hideous black tie to be admitted. Williams wore dark glasses to cover his eyes, which were bothered by the pollution in the air.

At lunch we spoke about Carson McCullers ("She was the best writer, baby. We used to sit at the same table, I on one side, and Carson on the other, and work together. She was the only writer I knew I could work with"), and about the antiwar and revolutionary movements in the United States, in which Williams's fierce interest had not been numbed by the experience of the benefit. His interest was growing while mine was declining. And we talked about death. Tennessee told stories about old friends dying of cancer, and for some reason clear to neither of us we found our own peril before death hysterically funny.

I told Tennessee about my disillusionment with activism. And I returned to the subject of the theft of the benefit money, about which I was still bitter. "How can you make a revolution if you can't trust your friends?"

"I don't know. But somehow they happen."

Somehow. Maybe friendships in the movement were precarious because they were contingent on matters beyond their control—on temporary organization, on tactics, on ideology constantly shifting from one polarity to the next. And therefore they were in a real sense contingent upon the mutual acceptance of a political line. What friendship could not sustain was political disagreement because all political questions became questions of loyalty, and disagreement was taken personally. How can you live like that?

While my friendship with Tennessee was based in part on a sharing of a common political faith that was left wing and radical (although I suspected that he was fundamentally farther to the left than I), its primary dynamic was a high mutual dependency, a nearly identical sense of humor, and an understanding of the function of the writer as being intimately related to his personal survival, to salvation. What struck me as peculiar was that while I was more and more desirous of shedding my direct, physical involvement in political actions in favor of greater commitment to writing, Williams was seemingly becoming increasingly interested in political activity and less in his role as a playwright.

So in that regard, at that time, we were as well paired as two warriors in the ancient games, for in our loud friendship we fed and renewed each other's hunger for a slight but important shift in the balance of our lives and commitments. And where Tennessee was different from me in terms of his role, in how he understood himself as a writer, was his age (twice mine) and the fact that in his life long ago he had resolved the questions facing me. And the answers he drew were inapplicable to my life.

11

In February, several weeks before I left New York, the Russian poet Yevtushenko arrived to begin his American tour. I had never met him, although I had, at great distance, enormous respect for him, arising largely out of the courage I believed he displayed in the poem "Babi Yar," and in his criticism of the Warsaw Pact invasion of Czechoslovakia. He was a man who apparently had resolved the dilemma so many of us faced: How does one balance socialism with the writer's need of freedom? Therefore I saw him as an alternative, a socialist writer who had somehow struck the correct balance. He seemed a survivor to me, and that was the nature of the question facing me: How does one survive?

Yevtushenko was a writer and a socialist humanist in a country, the Soviet Union, which I considered social fascist and imperialist. His position vis-à-vis the party was in many ways comparable to that of writers everywhere on the left to their native revolutionary movements. Or at least so I believed. And if you were a writer on the left and believed the revolution was inevitable, you had a morbid curiosity about how writers functioned in post-revolutionary states. Which was, in effect, given the eschatology of the left, a concern over how your future as a writer would be lived. The revolution had occurred in the Soviet Union, and there, fifty years later, was this poet speaking out against its abuses. That seemed heroic

commissar zhenya

to me. And if the experience of "intellectual workers" in the Soviet Union and in Cuba, for example, did not give one much cause for rejoicing, nevertheless Yevtushenko, as a poet who held many socialist beliefs with the rest of us, stood as evidence that poetry could survive unbought after the revolution.

Ruth Ford brought me to meet Yevtushenko at a party given in his honor by Mr. and Mrs. H. J. Heinz. Their duplex apartment overlooked the East River. It was a large affair, many people from the arts invited, and yet curiously there were no representatives from the party or from the left present except for myself and one other writer. Perhaps that was not so odd, not so odd anyway as the connection between the Soviet poet and the Heinz family, certainly a premier dynasty among the American economic royalists. Mrs. Heinz was an editor of the literary review *Antaeus*, and the Heinz family had given the city of Pittsburgh the concert hall where "Yevtushenko and Friends," his road show, was to be staged.

I arrived at the party full of enthusiasm about this man who was an example of how a writer could maintain his integrity, his political voice, without giving over to party dictates—in short, a man who was both a socialist and a free poet and thus an alternative to street activism. And, too, my enthusiasm came from the sense of solidarity, almost a proprietary feeling, I experienced in the presence of other socialists whether I knew them personally or not. He is *like* me, I thought.

Warren Beatty, Ruth Ford, and I rode the elevator to the Heinz apartment in the company of Yevtushenko and his "translator." The presence of the "translator" bothered me and caused my sympathy for Yevtushenko to swell. I have seen enough visiting Russian culture heroes to spot the KGB or the CIA in their omnipresent companions. And I have been trailed enough by police agents—Chicago was especially given to expending police labor in trailing unimportant leftists—to realize the degree of courage it took not to be inhibited by them. It took an act of will. I may be wrong about his "translator"; however, I never saw Yevtushenko in New York without one on his heels, which increasingly struck me as ominous, since he spoke perfect English. In fact, it was only when the occasion appeared to suit him, usually at public readings and interviews, that he fell into a thick, guttural, nearly unintelligible Russian-accented English. But perhaps that was part of the act.

Yevtushenko was dressed in a sweater and baggy trousers. He was a tall man, lanky, rather All-American farmboy in appearance as if he had just come in on the Greyhound from the Great Plains; his hair was light in color and cut Marine-short; his skin was very pale and rather pasty in texture. At the party he was melodramatic, loquacious, overbearing, intense, conceited, possessing enormous stamina and acute cleverness. People told me with amazement that he made do on very little sleep, drank heavily all night, and rose early for long days of television appearances, poetry readings, interviews, and walking tours, only to finish the evening with more drinking. A truly Siberian endurance. Around him I felt like a *Pravda* caricature of the dissipated, effete Western intellectual.

During this period the American press was filled with criticism of the Soviet Union, attacking its persecution of the Jews, its suppression of writers, its expansionist foreign policy. I did not like the Soviet Union, since I do not like oppression, yet in some way I, like other American leftists, found myself continually stuck with it, like gum on the sole of one's shoe, and we were always being asked to answer for its excesses. We did not feel in any way responsible for the Soviets; most of us in the New Left considered them little better than state capitalists. However, they were nominally socialist, and one had to take the good with the bad.

Therefore, I asked Yevtushenko how it was that he was free to travel and speak out when so many of his fellow Soviet writers languished in labor camps and in "psychiatric" wards and were barred from travel and publication. I was not the only one to press him on that point. He was asked similar questions many times until he finally refused to answer, accusing his questioner instead of having been produced in the same "anti-Soviet factory" as the other anti-Communist critics. It did not apply. I was not anti-Communist.

In reply to me, he said, "You Americans. It is so simple for you. You do not understand us. You know little about survival. I am the greatest poet in Russia. It is a difficult thing for the government to put me in jail. I am too *cunning*." He tapped his head with his finger. In Moscow, he continued by way of illustration, he was stopped by a policeman for drunken driving. Instead of arresting him, the policeman implored him to drive home carefully for the "little poet" was too precious to the Russian people to risk his life.

None of which really answered my question. Here I was thinking I was his brother, both of us writers and socialists, and he was giving me a lot of evasive nonsense.

"But what about the imprisoned writers? What about the Jews?"

He squinted and then rested his hand on my arm. I was wearing a red SDS button with the words "Smash Imperialism" and a clenched fist imprinted on it. He fingered the button. "Smash imperialism, you see?" It was so simple. "That is Vietnam, my friend."

And that was not an answer either.

Later that night someone said to him, "You are the greatest poet in Russia!"

Yevtushenko was sitting at a round table eating. He looked up, visibly offended. "No, *du monde!* I am also the greatest living Russian actor. They want to give me a prize as the greatest actor. But the government says No, please Zhenya, you cannot also have that! That is too much for us to give you. A prize for the greatest poet, yes, Zhenya. But as an actor, too? That would give you too much power, the people love you already too much!"

One more note about the Heinz party. A trivial incident

occurred which illustrated something about the poet and something about me. What it said about me was that I was very naïve to find the incident surprising. When Yevtushenko walked into the Heinz apartment, Mrs. Heinz informed him that they had imported Russian vodka on ice if he cared for some.

"Vodka!" he exclaimed, shocked. *"Champagne!* French! *Brut! Très brut!"* He seemed accustomed to giving orders. That was the commissar in him, I thought.

I attended the first performance of "Yevtushenko and Friends," at Madison Square Garden's Felt Forum. It was one of the most appalling evenings of theater I have experienced, and I have been to a lot of bombs. First, the "Friends" were not his friends, not in the sense that word is commonly understood. Rather they were well-intentioned writers—Dickey, Kunitz, and others—and hack actors and musicians who were brought together to give dramatic (actually melodramatic, indeed histrionic) form to his verse. James Dickey was rightly embarrassed by the background music. A chorus of squeaky-clean, overly enthusiastic, Bloomingdale's "hippies" whose idea of musical background was to shout in sing-song the most banal lines in Yevtushenko's banal verse. Dickey laughed when he read a love poem because the piano player began tinkling on the keys notes sounding like birds chirping. Well, it probably went over big in Minsk.

Eugene McCarthy, another "Friend," refused to read the Yevtushenko poem assigned to him by one of the "translators," dismissing the verse as "shit." Instead he read a poem of his own. It was quite lovely. He walked on the stage alone and quickly exited, but not before the athletic Yevtushenko trapped him in an awkward embrace in midexit for the benefit of the press photographers. McCarthy looked astonished and indignant.

Most of the reading of the Russian's work was done either by Yevtushenko himself in his heaviest Russian accent, with his arms flailing the air, his voice rising and falling like a bear in heat, his eyes rolling heavenward, or by an English actor named, improbably enough, Barry Boys. Only Mr. Boys could outwail, outrumble, outweep Yevtushenko in the histrionics competition. This is Soviet art? I thought. This is the flower of the revolution?

Mr. Boys was dressed in a flowing black blouse with puffy Elizabethan sleeves, black tight trousers and shiny boots, and the campiest Greenwich Avenue belt with a Hollywood Boulevard rhinestone buckle all aglitter in the blue and pink Las Vegas lights. A breathy youth ran out to the microphone and shouted, "The poet! The *poet!* The POET!"—Yevtushenko wandered out to receive applause—and Mr. Boys leaped to the stage, placed one hand on his waist, spread his legs, arched his back, tilted his head dramatically toward the heavens, and began emoting verse like a high-school drama major trying out for a part on the soaps. It was embarrassing. Not for Yevtushenko—he reveled in it—but for the audience who had paid outrageous sums to be taken to the cleaners by the socialist poet, the audience who, after the light began to dawn, started booing and leaving the site of the travesty.

I kept wondering why he had come to the United States when many other socialist intellectuals—most prominently Sartre—refused to come as long as the Indochina War continued? Money? Yes. Publicity? That too. Fundamentally, I concluded, he was sent here to deflect American criticism over the persecution of the Jews and the suppression of intellectual freedom in the Soviet Republics. He handled his assignment magnificently. He wrapped himself in "Babi Yar" the way Nixon wrapped himself in "Old Glory." And he cynically exploited the bombing of Sol Hurok's Manhattan offices by the Jewish Defense League to deflect Jewish-American criticism of anti-Semitism in the Soviet Union onto outrage over the tactics of those who opposed it. It was as if an American in Russia attacked antiwar demonstrators in the Soviet Union for their tactics rather than dealing with the actual question of American aggression. It was an old ploy. He accused the Jewish Defense League of anti-Semitism. I have little use for the JDL, but that is absurd. And yet to a large degree he was able to sell that patent nonsense. "Babi Yar" again.

Yevtushenko was dying to meet President Nixon, no easy task. How was he to arrange it? By chance he learned that Senator and Mrs. Jacob Javits were giving a party for presidential adviser Henry Kissinger. Warren Beatty was among the invited. (Beatty was already on Yevtushenko's program as one of the "Friends," although Beatty had the good sense not to appear at Felt Forum.) Yevtushenko tried contacting Beatty, and then he called Peter Glenville. Glenville reached Mrs. Javits and arranged an invitation for Yevtushenko.

There were several cruel ironies to the incident, beyond the obvious one of the Soviet poet supping with the architect of American war policy on the eve of the Philip Berrigan trial. Two things occurred at the Javits affair which seemed most telling to me about the character of Yevtushenko and, through him, about the character of socialism and the "New Man" in the Soviet Republics. And together they reinforced my cynicism about the Communist party and those portions of the left it influenced . . . for I had once flirted with the party and therefore this cynicism was painful to me.

When Yevtushenko entered the Senator's Park Avenue apartment he stopped and glanced around the room and then announced in a loud voice, "There are too many goddamn Jews in here!" His remark was heard by at least six witnesses. No one chided him for his racist shout.

At dinner he sat himself beside Henry Kissinger and begged him for an invitation to the White House. The great Russian Communist removed his wristwatch and presented it to Kissinger, saying, "I give it with my deepest respect and love." Mr. Kissinger, eager to accommodate, accepted it happily and promised the poet seventy minutes alone with the President.

"He is a clever man." It was several weeks after the Yevtushenko visit, and several of us were talking about him.

One of the women closely involved in his American tour was speaking. "He is tough and clever. And he despises us. He knew he could make an anti-Semitic remark at the Javitses' and get away with it. He knew he could go around the country attacking America and refuse to accept criticism of Russian oppression and the rest. His own stinking role in Russia. I guess it's because he senses we're weak. Good old American masochists. Oh, Christ, I bet the bastard's having a bloody good laugh on all of us. He'll go back to Russia and tell his cronies what bloody fools the Americans are, what saps. He comes over here and everyone lines up to kiss his Russian backside. It's too disgusting."

Looking back, it seemed we were always making excuses for Yevtushenko, as we made them for Angela Davis and how many others whose politics and public lives were filled with inconsistencies, whose outrage was inhumanly selective and muted by the imprint of the party's thumb. By "we" I mean those of us on the left, some who met him privately. It was shameful that I and others who had the opportunity did not confront him more aggressively with his complicity, putatively through silence (although who knows what quiet bargaining, what political buying and selling went on in the Soviet Union between the official writers and the commissars who police them), his complicity in the persecution of the Jews and the suppression of intellectual freedom in the Soviet Fatherland. And still the question: Why was he free and his countrymen in jail? Why did he have two foreign cars and a dacha while fellow writers had barbed wire and silence in the ice? In America it was becoming acceptable if not fashionable in some leftist intellectual circles to be mildly anti-Zionist and to indulge in a tolerance of anti-Semitism. We rationalized it among blacks. We understated it among the Russians, appealing to their long and criminal history of pogrom and racial murder, to the more recent political complications and suspicions arising from Israeli military policy. We were wrong to rationalize evil.

It was confusing to me. Perhaps, as Yevtushenko said, we

Westerners were decadent. Perhaps the West was perverted. Maybe it was our decadence that made us "oversensitive" to the "social disciplining" of Soviet writers guilty of the sin of "formalism." ("Formalism" was one of the charges Yevtushenko hurled at Solzhenitsyn.) I think he would have said that we had a misplaced sympathy for writers who violated the Marxist-Leninist orthodoxy of Socialist Realism in the arts. Maybe they are counterrevolutionary, closet bourgeois, acting through their art to advance lines objectively contrary to the building of communism and the necessary dictatorship of the proletariat. Maybe not.

I was confused. Because I was a socialist and also a believer in human freedom. It was, in fact, the commitment to freedom that led me inevitably to socialism. However, I perceived a difference between democratic socialism and Soviet social fascism. Regrettably, it was finally not the soul of socialism that Yevtushenko heard singing. It was the spirit of social fascism. His poetry reeked of false values and cheap romanticism, the same qualities characteristic of the falsely heroic paintings, the Great Patriotic War canvases, the toiling proletariat propaganda posters that Soviet organs commissioned under Stalin and continue to commission today. Yevtushenko had the heart of a Soviet functionary, and the degree to which it commanded him was the exact degree to which he was an enemy of socialism and human freedom. I understood that at last. The gangsters had taken over the revolution and sent us their poets.

If that was true, then how was I to explain his seemingly authentic moments of courage: the criticism of the Warsaw Pact invasion, and his poem "Babi Yar"? I concluded that they were explained by the same motivation that accounted for his appointment to the board of the Soviet Union of Writers, which acted as a disciplining bureau for Soviet thought, and his silence on the jailing of fellow poets and the persecution of the Jews and other religious and cultural minorities. It was careerist opportunism that animated his moments of apparent heroism. His first commitment was to himself, to his career: his massive conceit and egotism seemed evidence of the strength of that commitment. Second, and this was only a guess, I suspected that he maintained a commitment to the party bureaucracy, or at least to that section of it favorable to his own advancement. Yet even that I thought he betrayed.

When an American bourgeois writer, such as myself, criticized American aggression and war crimes in Indochina, when he struggled against racism and repression at home, he did not betray his values. On the contrary, his criticism sprang from what remained of humanism and libertarian bias in bourgeois thought. But when a Soviet writer, an official "socialist," a Communist, when he remained silent on the suppression of human liberty in his own country fifty years *after* the revolution, he betrayed not only the future of his country but socialism and the revolution as well.

I came away from Yevtushenko's American visit sick at heart. He stayed too long, long enough for my suspicions to be confirmed, for the myth of his intellectual independence and moral integrity to be dissipated, long enough to see him as a Cold Warrior not yet come in from the cold; to see him as a loser, a man of bad faith, a poseur, a stalking horse for Soviet imperialism. He was not a friend of freedom, nor a true socialist. And that admission cut out from under me one more myth that bound me sentimentally if no other way to the old left.

I spoke with Allen Ginsberg during this time and expressed my disillusionment with Yevtushenko. Ginsberg, trying to justify the moral ambivalence of the man, said, "He is trying his best to unify the Russian-American Soul under the banner of poesy; in heaven great golden thrones of credit are given for good intentions." Well, Ginsberg was wrong. And Sartre correct. Intentions count for nothing. They are not worth a bucket of spit. And besides, it was precisely Yevtushenko's intentions that seemed most wrong to me.

Yevtushenko wrote of being a man shuttling between the

city of "yes" and the city of "no," by which he meant New York and Moscow. He referred to his being a courier crossing the ice to deliver messages from one side to the other. In a love poem he wrote, "I sped back and forth in a sick panic, with a hard-hit mask of a face, with a mind split two ways, both ways false." I thought, on reading that: "Yevtushenko's ability to act as the courier, the mail boat, between two sides was due to his extraordinary capacity to be many things to many men." In a word, to be unprincipled.

After Yevtushenko had his meeting with the President, I asked Ginsberg how he could have respect for a man who would sit and lend his reputation to a President considered a war criminal by the socialist camp. Ginsberg mumbled something about "sentient beings" and how poets must reach everyone, even war criminals.

His answer struck me as evangelical nonsense. One of the few resources poets owned was their command of a special integrity. At their finest they were moral teachers. When Robert Lowell refused dinner at the White House he made an important moral statement. In part the poet's, the writer's, function was to withdraw moral support and to place ethical sanctions against people who committed criminal acts in the name of the People. That is a priestly function that belongs, probably by default, to the poet. In that sense his life, as a conduit for moral suasion, is subversive of fraud and states built on falseness. Free poets and writers are always among the first to be jailed, their books banned. What Yevtushenko did in seeking the meeting with Nixon was to give, by his presence, the stamp of respectability to murder. And that was criminal, considering what Yevtushenko was for us on the left.

I should not have been surprised by Yevtushenko's action. It was appropriate. It fitted him. Zhenya was bequeathed to us by the Cold War. Poets have their uses to tyrants. Verse too can be a weapon of state. Yevtushenko's tragedy was that he had not the courage to resist the euphoria of nearness to power. He would rather be a doorkeeper in the House of the Lord, rubbing shoulders with the ruling class, accepting their smiles, than be a free voice. Egomania betrayed him. He believed his press clippings. Now history has passed him. He was of the fifties, his poetry and his politics. He belonged in a room exchanging polite banter with Richard Nixon.

12

Yevtushenko angered me because he believed that the Soviet Union was the end product of the struggle of mankind for liberty, that all the sacrifice and labor of the left throughout the world, by people much braver and more decent than he or I—their lives cut off too soon for the sake of freedom—that all that effort and costly hope was spent to bring the model of Soviet communism to a benighted earth. The only response I could have to such conceit and falseness was contempt and anger, for I do not think that either he or his compatriots in the regime were worth being counted among the ranks of the sons of liberty, an honorable term, certainly not among those I had been privileged to know in the movement. Good God, even the punks who ripped us off were better than Zhenya. At least their anguish and their young, confused struggle were more committed and real than anything he was or claimed to represent.

I say that because of what I know was paid by the radical young in America. Certainly I knew many young people on the left who found their way disastrously into drugs or helplessly into jail or some other end nothing in their youth hinted at, so many wasted in so short a time that I am still baffled by the loss, unable to summon the reasons for their undoing, why they failed or died or went underground, inactivated, as good as dead, lingering pur-

*the horse
of horses*

poselessly in a drug haze between jail and exile. And yet they were better than Zhenya. By far.

It was remarkable how strong I felt during the sixties in New York as I watched so many break around me, crashing on the Lower East Side or the Upper West in defensive apathy, where Seconal and amyl nitrite and mescaline are better ways to kill the memory than communism, and codeine and smack and Preludin and coke better highs above defeat than Mao, no, better than life. It finally arrived for me, although I was far down the line, and the irony was that I discovered myself appealing to the same cheap tonics, too easy, which debilitated or killed my friends when they ran out of answers. Maybe, as Yevtushenko believed, the party was a better place to run to than Quāālude shot with strychnine. It's all the same in the end, total loss. Then I watched my friends with alarm and sadness and, yes, contempt, thinking they were losers without balls, exceptions, unfit. They were neither.

It was immediately after seeing Yevtushenko that Jann Eller entered my life again, via letter; Eller who, more than anyone else, represented, in its finest personification, the committed revolutionary. And when I heard from him, read what he told me in his letter, then the possibility of that alternative faded for good, and I was on my own. No more revolutionary dreams dancing in my head. If Jann Eller, younger, twenty-six when I last saw him, could not bend life to him but was broken by it, then I could not make it by the route he chose. The letter was a crucial imposition on my life. I thought Jann would survive. He didn't.

Eller was the kind of person I most wanted to be. He was a young revolutionary of great courage and intelligence, possessed of charm and grace and style, as a great painting is, naturally. He just grew that way. He was committed to undertaking any means necessary to overthrow a system he believed unjust and deadly to his friends. Only, unlike many others, he never became callous and unfeeling.

I think Eller failed because he had nothing outside the

movement to sustain him when the troubles came, no network of friends and interests outside politics to support him when politics failed. He grew isolated within the movement, when he was facing prison and most needed friends, isolated by the very political developments that delivered him to it. His political history was that of someone continually moving left, and with each shift came arguments and erosion in friendship, separating him more and more from the centrist majority until he reached the place where he was alone and beyond help. He had nothing but the movement. He had too much pride or commitment to retrace his steps. He would not ask for help until it was too late, would not accept it when it was offered, not ask for it because help meant compromise in political attitude, and he could not bring himself to compromise when his politics had cost him so much. So there he was, an activist when mass activism was over, fighting on alone. A revolutionary without friends. And when the troubles came he shattered into drugs.

He was an alternative, Eller was. The committed activist. When he broke, the option died.

The day after the Heinz party for Yevtushenko I received this letter from Jann.

I carry a sawed-off shotgun at all times taped to my thigh . . . is that really so bad, Dotson? The influence, I mean . . . my friends are as follows . . . dope dealers and acid heads and chicks that pull me down farther than I've ever yet dropped my trousers . . . what then is left, Dotson? Am I what the dopers down the street tell me I am? An honest to goodness barb freak . . . my best friend is forty-five, on the lam from [a] State Penitentiary, contracted hepatitis from Richard's dirty needle last week . . . dirty Richard . . . what a shame . . . for a smack freak to lend out dirty needles . . . you see, Dotson, Dave was in prison for seventeen years, he's a blackman mechanic and all of a sudden one day says to me, Pig, I'm going to make you my partner . . . so no longer am I allowed to rub noses with the sea shells out along the Pacific beaches . . . I gotta take this lousy cocksucker with me . . . and my chick says, Dave is the most honest guy in the world and along with it she stashes my reds and yellows under the sea shells she knows where my nose hasn't been. . . . All these nites I've been having dreams, Dotson . . . that Roy Rogers will lend me the horse of horses to make my rounds . . . all the time, like a merry-go-round . . . constantly I'm on the move, Dotson . . . my raft tumbles from one doper's pad to another . . . I'm wanted everywhere . . . I don't own my name anymore . . . sure, you're right . . . the mousey-eyed landlords do look mousey . . . but, tricks of the trade are not tough to pick up with partners like Dave . . . whaddya say to that . . . a good boy turned bad . . . fuck the revolution . . . fuck it all . . . let me be a capitalist dope-hound and turn the money over to you for research on the ulcer problem . . . say hello to Frankie, Tommy, Jack, Brian, Tennessee, they'll all be rich as shit someday too . . . tell me, Dotson, are you happy to hear that the last of the puritans is out of the fog? Dotson, I'm not afraid anymore! We'll drink and drink and drink and plug up your ulcers . . . maybe even with smack. . . .

The following day a shirt I had given him came in the mail. I put it on and wore it all day, walking down the street in the afternoon sunshine and looking down at myself, at my chest and stomach beneath the cloth, thinking it was he. For the shirt, like a life mask, reminded me of him, of the day I gave it to him in Chicago at the last convention of the student left.

He had so much going for him, sensitivity and intelligence and commitment. It was not enough.

I remember traveling to Erie, Pennsylvania, to visit Jann. He had been released from prison in Illinois weeks before. Tom Seligson and I stayed the night at his place and the following day he took us around his old neighborhood. Small, wooden bungalows in disrepair, housing the families of unskilled black and white workers. On the corners, by the food stores and drug outlets, their teen-age sons loitered in the heat of the day talking big. A matter of time and they would follow their fathers into the factories and mines. Jann left his city to organize in Chicago and on the Coast, but he never broke with his neighborhood, with his past. He never had to, because his people were the concern of the struggle, and he was proud of them. He never lost the capacity to feel for the powerless in America.

Perhaps he felt too much. Or was beaten once too often, or faced jail one time too many and was alone—and then the drugs were there offering the end to feeling. I do not know.

I remember walking the filthy shores of Lake Erie with him, the public beaches closed because rich men dumped poison into the lake (it was the cheapest way).

"They have nowhere to swim when the beaches are shut. That's why they hang around and get hooked." He was speaking of his friends and younger brothers.

"Where do the rich swim?"

"They got their pools." He smiled. "I'd sure like to swim in their pools." He was quiet for a time.

We strolled up the beach with our shirts off, sweating in the heat, his long blond hair blowing in the wind. He kicked stones or hurled them skidding across the surface of the lake.

"Someday," he said.

"Someday what?"

"Someday we all will." He laughed loudly, throwing his head back, as if he had made the funniest and most absurd remark.

"Someday we'll what?"

"Swim in them pools."

Banal memory, working-class youth dreaming of swimming in the pools of the rich when his lake had been despoiled. Fuck it, it was that sentiment, the desire to end privilege, that made him beautiful. It was so natural for him, his politics, and its naturalness, the uncontrived, un-affected quality of his commitment, was as graceful and elegant as the gesture—the arc of his arm, the flick of his wrist—he made in sending the stones hopping across the water. I hated the rich. He didn't. I wonder why.

I have told all this because the alternative represented by Eller was not only that of activism outside the organized movement. (He was the revolutionary-as-loner.) More, it was the possibilities of friendship, specifically those created in the movement. I am trying to get to the bottom of it be-cause I am now convinced that it was those friendships, the possibilities of them, what they provided in terms of honor and loyalty and the employment of courage, manhood, which called me into political activism; or if not the cause of my involvement, they were certainly what kept me there. The movement, that web of friendship, was the only com-munity I ever knew.

Eller went with me to Mailer's party at the Whitney Museum following the showing of his movie *Maidstone*. Mailer talked with Eller and was impressed by him, I sup-pose by the integrity underlying his handsome face.

"Who's the leader of the pack?" Mailer asked. I pointed to Jann. He was the best I ever met in the movement.

So the best failed.

I called a number of friends on the Coast after receiving the letter. No one knew where he was. "I think he O.D.ed," one of them told me. Too soon.

Somehow all the lies or fantasies or uncompleted dreams or loves that held me to the movement, which I used like shoddy patchwork to hide reality from myself, were bound up in him, in the longing for male union, the most danger-ous kind of sentiment. Certainly I sought much in Jann. I would look at him and say, not that we *would* win, but that we *deserved* to win. Or at least he did. He was better than anybody on the other side. I know I am getting sloppy here, I am becoming sentimental. I do not care. His life had such an enormous effect on mine. I loved him, you see, and that makes it difficult to write about him without pity over what I avoided and he could not, over what I have lost in losing him. He wrote me when I was on the edge of cracking up, beginning the slide into booze and drugs. And his letter was the push that sent me down. He was the one loss I could not take. In a way it is a shameful thing to admit, because it speaks so blatantly of weakness. Listen, he was worth more than the movement to me, and to have saved him from harm, from what overtook him, I would have renounced it all, thrown it over, sided against what I was to save him. He was beyond help. When he broke, it took from activism its romance. And I was left on the beach without him.

Gradually I began turning toward other things, drugs I guess, and away from life. I became detached, depersonalized, as if I stood outside myself watching the game. I hurt inside. I think where the *conscious* turning away started was in Baltimore, when the slide became inevitable, after the loss of Jann.

part three

THE
JOURNEY
DOWN

13

I was invited to speak to medical students at Johns Hopkins University in Baltimore on "the political uses of violence." I had written occasionally on the subject, and my interest in direct action had shifted to the psychological motivations behind it as my personal taste for or need of it waned.

To go back a moment: while I was a committed radical, I was beginning to accept somewhat the statement *The New Leader* had once made about me, that I was a "patrician radical," meaning that my political commitment had more to do with circumstance and educated feelings of obligation than with any real Marxist conviction. Certainly I had no understanding of economics and little of history. In short, I was beginning to see my erratic antiwar activities as having arisen out of a contempt for middle-class values which led me into alliance with any group in opposition to them, and out of a need to establish manhood aggressively, through violence. While my violence (too strong a word) of the bar-fight variety, for example, tended to be extremely muted of late, I believed that manhood involved mastery and command: one fought to possess its turf as one possessed a woman. The possession of it was always provisional and contingent upon the next act, the next confrontation, in which one gambled something of ultimate value.

What I spoke about at Johns Hopkins was the radical

cowboys

left and the relative probability of revolution within advanced industrial countries and, specifically, about what limits I believed ought to be applied by the revolutionary left in the United States to its own employment of violence. Standing before several hundred medical students in an auditorium named after John Kennedy (an obscene irony) and analyzing the future uses of violence by the left, their appropriateness or need of it, their situationalist productivity or lack of it, there came a point at which it did not make sense anymore. It was a senselessness similar to what I had felt listening to Yevtushenko equivocate evasively on the question of freedom in the Soviet Union. No, it was similar to what I felt in watching homosexual pornography: I could understand the causes of it, indeed the necessity for it, but it had little meaning to me. It went nowhere I wanted to go. There were adequate reasons for political violence, but what was senseless was my speaking about it there, before people whose interest was largely technical and scientific, as in observation studies of the pathology of deranged rats. Laboratory animals, and I was the selected guide. There was an absurdity to it. What I was talking about was wholly remote from the situation. Its meaningfulness was not at the university but in the streets. My speech, the response to it, the questions asked, the liberal disdain of a largely smug and comfortable audience, my own super-butch pose—I wore a biker's leather jacket and boots, a cowboy hat—my profanity, the entire tough shtick was contrived. It was bad theater. The longer the session lasted, the more depersonalized and self-conscious I became, and the more convinced I was that I should have become what I always wanted to become, ever since I was a kid at the El Lago Theater: a cowboy actor.

The week before Johns Hopkins, I had seen my agent in New York about getting into a B-grade Hollywood Western. I wanted to be a cowboy in a real cowboy movie (I was too hopelessly, ineptly urban to make it work as a real cowboy outside the movies), the kind of stuff Hoot Gibson and Guy

Madison and William Boyd were in where the dumb stud always gives up the ranch owner's daughter to ride off into the dust on his horse alone, or with (if he's lucky) a compatible buddy.

"All I want," I told my agent, "is a walk-on role, like where I saunter into a saloon cactus-dry and slap my hand against the bar, you know, giving a fuck-you look to the tenderfoots and desert-rot in the place, and say, 'Make it a whiskey. *Straight.* And make it pronto.' Or maybe I could do a scene where I sit at a table playing cards and at the slightest hint of cheating I murder or pistol-whip the cheating sonofabitch." Natch.

Speaking at the university about violence, I wanted to be away in a movie, to be able finally to hitch up my trousers at New York parties, at dull political meetings, and announce it was all bullshit over my head, it was unclean, that I was simply a cowboy actor who also wrote, and thus dissociate myself from the New York tenderfoots and from an intellectual community that seemed to me to be losing touch with the America out there beyond the Hudson. Losing touch, as I was losing touch. And frightened, or rather disquieted, by the loss.

All the time I spoke, a group of high-school-age kids sat in the front row watching me. They were from East Baltimore, a racially mixed, hopelessly impoverished community of dark streets and decaying houses where a large number of people lived the kind of life that made most American cities a national disgrace. East Baltimore had the highest infant mortality rate, the lowest per capita income, the greatest crime rate coupled with the most corrupt police, the highest incidence of drug addiction, the highest unemployment, the worst schools, the worst housing, and a despair as intolerable as it was involuntary.

After the speech a party was given for me at a professor's house in an upper-income, tight-security housing compound. About thirty people were at the party. I was tired—it was my third speech in two days—and I was drinking heavily. I ended in the kitchen several hours later, leaning against the sink as half a score of terribly bright, terribly sincere, intense, purer-than-thou, leftist students went at me for my decadence, whatever that meant to them. It meant, I guess, that I displayed no guilt over the happy fact that I was not in jail and still alive, whereas, if I were really principled, I should have been a jailed corpse.

Into the kitchen came a youth, named Derek. And in not wanting to, he broke me.

Derek had been at the speech at the University. He believed it, took it seriously, could not tell the pretense from the pain, the dancer from the dance. Uninvited, he came to the party at the professor of psychiatry's house. He had never been in such a house. He had dropped out of school in the eighth grade. He had been to reformatory twice. He made his bread at burglary and pushing. He spoke to me and told me that he, Derek, wanted to become active in the movement. "What movement?" I should have asked. But that would have served no good purpose.

"I can't take the shit no more. My brother and me, you know, we live on East Baltimore Street. He got knifed. Most guys I know are on drugs. It ain't no life. I think we got to blow it up."

"What up?"

"The fucking country."

"That's not easy to do." I was at a loss for an answer.

"I could kill easy," he boasted. "I got nothing to lose."

Derek was handsome to me, looking almost exactly like the actor who played in the British movie *The Leather Boys*. And the actor (Reggie) looked and bore the accents of Derek, poor white, of every street-punk, half-assed, jiving drugstore cowboy, only Derek was a hillbilly from Carolina via West Virginia, which is near to being a cowboy in attitude and style, near as nylon is to silk. He had a soft, Southeastern accent and bad grammar and a syntax so individualistic, so authentically his own, that as a writer I cannot hope to re-create it. But it was a handsome thing to hear.

Derek, growing intimate, took off his shirt and showed me knife scars on the left side under his collar bone, and another scar on the lower part of his back above the left buttock. "Got 'em in a fight at the Dillard Houses [public projects]. Some of the blacks was leaning on a chick. You gotta protect your own."

When he removed his shirt I remembered Jann Eller stripping for the photographers at a party on the roof one summer in Manhattan.

In the kitchen several people argued about the war, Derek listening, watching me like wolf eyes by a campfire, making me nervous.

Derek said, "You know so much. You tell me what to do."

I was stoned by now, and I could only lean and stare as Derek moved at me, telling me in a rush that his cousin just wrote him from the war and his best buddy had been blown apart inches from him, and his brains "runs down his chest, they runs down his chest. . . ." Derek was drunk himself, and like some crazy mariner stumbling in unbidden, refusing to leave off, he kept tossing the image of that death around the room.

What he was demanding of me was the easy end of the war that had taken his cousin's best friend. He wanted that horror righted and made accountable, and somehow by that peculiar authority that attaches itself to a writer at a party, he held me in the net, responsible. I would not accept responsibility. Never again. I would give no more advice. I wanted no more kids like Eller and how many others in a decade to watch in their dash toward violence and self-destruction, to see them become fugitives busted, beat down, run through, burnt out. No, I had enough guilt. I would say no more. There was no easy end to anything. I wanted no more shirts sent to me in the mail like sweaty remnants from a distant war.

"Tell me what to do."

What I had settled for then, like every American boy, was to be well liked, not to be bothered, and, when spaced by fatigue or booze or angel dust, to be given the benefit of the doubt. I could think of nothing to say to Derek that was at all sufficient. The platitudes I had mouthed since the early sixties had become patently inadequate, so detached from actuality that Derek would have laughed if I had laid them on him. For what did they have to do with the end his cousin witnessed? He would rightly think I was putting him on.

For two hours the kid bugged me, and I kept saying, "What the goddamn hell do you want from me?" I knew he was putting the hustle on me. Finally, he had clearly sensed what every radical writer I ever met who was at the game long enough and had enough self-honesty to admit it to himself knew: we were riddled by guilt; we could never do enough in an age of action to justify the essential passivity of writing. Like them all, I got flashes in the middle of the night that somewhere unwittingly the defenses had broken and through the breach all the posturing and repetitive rhetoric had been seen as profoundly false. For we had all chosen, too comfortably, to make ourselves into what we had become. And what I knew, what Derek did not catch, not then, was the helpless mendacity of my present politics and life. I was a literary-political whore, a mercenary up for grabs; what motivated me in the gut was unreason, was sheer contrary rebellion. If the tables turned and I found myself by some crazy fluke within the ruling circles of any state at any time, I would slide irrevocably into opposition. In the Kingdom of Peace I would be a troublemaker. Unlike Derek, I was not born a victim in America, and yet I needed the existence of victims absolutely in order to make rebellion to become a man. And if there were no victims and no oppressor class I would have to create them. I hated straight values because they were the commanding, dominant values, not because I was especially oppressed by them. And there was something perverse in that, as perverse as it was necessary to the age.

Derek went through the party babbling of Vietnam until

he had caked it all in pall with the story of the guy's brains running. I was drawn to him, as I was to all rebellious youth, because he represented life. In time it would be taken from him. Like the cowboy, he was by nature, by the poverty of his means and education, his rank and manners, the futility of his hopes, the limitedness of his ambition; by all that he was unintentionally part of the resistance to the technotronic, postindustrial, dehumanized modern age. Because he had no place in it. By definition he was a loser.

I loved him for it, although I wanted no responsibility for his life. In a house filled with middle-liberal company students bent on working change through the system, and I the visiting party freak (I had the act memorized down to the exit lines), the kid was demanding the end to pretense and fraud, a response personal and direct outside the rhetoric. He was demanding *equality* with me, and that dated him. The old revolutions were about equality; ours concerned justice. There was the difference of a century between the two demands.

More and more, in the presence of underprivileged adolescents, I felt that I and my friends were phonies, bit actors out of work playing as if the house were stuffed with directors whose eyes were fixed on us like the eyes of fierce nuns upon a pope. Rhetoric had replaced reality. Compared to me, Derek's grip on life, on life forces, on the energy centers buckling life before themselves, in his grip, in his intimacy at that age with death, was reality. The contradiction and, if you will, the indictment of me was that his life was grounded in his easy violence and mine was not. His manly aggression was not forced, not contrived. I desired it, or maybe him in a way, because through it the jadedness was cut away and one was near to life.

I could not handle violence anymore. Nor give lectures on its uses. I had had more than a nodding acquaintance with it for years, pursuing it half drunk like some horny jock chasing women not for the sex but to disprove the impotence, and still it was foreign to me. It was imported into my life. I had chosen it. I was not born among the urban poor, where it was endemic, part of life. Maybe for that reason I had escaped paying for my flirtation. It was the kids who paid.

The following afternoon Derek showed me his neighborhood, and where he lived. He took me to a corner and pointed out the candy store in front of which his brother had been knifed to death.

"They dragged him over there." He gestured down the alley toward a brick wall. "See them garbage cans? They throwed him behind them. The garbage men found him in the morning."

14

I left Baltimore and flew to Los Angeles, where I was to write an article for *Esquire*. I was both paranoid and somewhat desperate in Los Angeles. I was beginning to take account of my life. It did not add up to much.

My paranoia was not helped by the fact that years before New York State had taken away my driver's license, leaving me trapped on the Coast, where pedestrian walking had become the monopoly of whores and encyclopedia salesmen. I lost my license when I crashed my Oldsmobile against a tree on the side of Highway 209 in the Catskills. While legally I was not responsible (I had swerved the car off the road to avoid another car passing into my lane), I had been using Phenaphen, a pain-killer that dulled my reflexes. The teen-age girl I had picked up at Vanilla Custer's Last Stand in Wurtzboro suffered a concussion, letting out a small cry of disbelief as we approached the tree. I never learned her name.

She stood behind me in line at the Custer Stand, and when I turned to leave I bumped into her, dropping my cone on the ground. We ended on the road, with the girl asking me if I was all right, of course, had I had too much to drink, of course not, I had had nothing to drink, and please don't drive so fast. And then the tree.

In court I paid for the tree, which was demolished along with the Oldsmobile. Unlike the car and the girl, it was not covered by insurance. My license was revoked.

running scared

What this serves to explain is not only my isolation in Los Angeles but something of my sexual tastes. The girl in the accident was fourteen years old, which is why she was in the car in the first place.

I had always liked young girls. It was the sense of violation I felt with them. They were not competitive. They were weak and unknowledgeable and I was able to get a sense of mastery and command with them I did not experience with older women. I felt the dominant male with whores and young girls. Even when they were not virgins, I liked to imagine them unbroken. It was the sense that I was corrupting them which was exciting. My sexual imagination depended upon the conviction that sex was sinful, a difficult concept to maintain but a necessary one for me. Mailer also believed that sex had no kick if it wasn't sinful. Being illegal helped too. Perhaps that was why homosexuality had a certain political appeal to me, why it seemed subversive and why I suspected that if it ever lost its status as outlawry it would lose its growing congregation of believers. It appealed, like rape, to the need of rebellion in men. I believed also that homosexuality, like rape, arose as a kind of volitional act out of early male hostility to the authority of women over their lives. In that sense it was a positive, i.e., subversive, state of being.

In Los Angeles I was fighting a writer's block and paranoia and a sense of defeat before life which was oppressive enough for me to wake in the middle of the night shivering in a cold sweat and pray, when I did not believe in prayer, that I would make it through the night.

Late one night I turned on the radio and picked up a Southern station and heard a gospel hymn. "I will meet you in the morning just inside the Eastern Gate. . . ." The promise in the sentiment was so great that I went out and bought the record the following morning when I had no phonograph to play it on.

That was one response to my being scared. Another, the usual one, was for me to sit earlier each afternoon in the bar at the Hyatt House on Sunset Strip and drink, avoiding going upstairs and working.

Or I would lie in the morning on a chaise longue beside the pool on the roof and watch the sun change the configurations of the houses dumped like hideous squatters across the banks of the Hollywood Hills. And I would think about the novels I wanted to write which I could not seem to start writing, about how or whether I could continue in any capacity in the movement, and about what appeared to be a sudden purposelessness to my life.

Several times I put through long-distance calls, once to Norman Mailer in Brooklyn, once to Peter Glenville, and once to Andy Warhol in Manhattan, and then, except for Warhol, refused to speak when the connection was made. Warhol I spoke with, because Warhol simply listened, saying, "Oh, really," refusing to acknowledge any sense of urgency, any lesion in his contrived placidity. "Oh, yes, uh . . . *fab*ulous."

One night I got drunk in a bar off Hollywood Boulevard and got into an argument with a union carpenter from Seattle about the war. Later we sat together at a table and complained about women, about life. Too much.

At night a melancholy. Three times I walked down Sunset Strip and bought a whore named Peg. A few words and she caught the nature of the game, giving me the line that this was her first time, she was desperate for money, her friends were addicts and it was my fault, prostitution was the only trade open in a capitalist country for unskilled women. On and on.

Peg was from Portland, very tall with small breasts, a long flat stomach and small hips, like a boy swimmer, and blond hair. She reminded me of a girl I had known in Westminster, Missouri, years before when I had traveled to the college as an SDS organizer. After speaking at the school, a group of overly healthy freshmen took me bowling and one of them introduced me to his sister, Lou Ann, who was a sophomore in high school. That night Lou Ann came over to my motel with her brother, and her brother got drunk, and Lou Ann took a bath, and I masturbated standing by the tub watching the soap bubbles slide down her small breasts.

In Los Angeles the whore named Peg sold me a packet of coke and the two of us snorted it, using a wooden popsicle stick to raise it like opaque dried sperm to our nostrils.

I lay naked on the bed. Peg sat with her legs spread on the chair opposite me. She was also naked. Her feet rested on the edge of the bed. I listened in a stoned haze, hearing her stories of young friends hooked, street angelics dying on bum trips from shit uncut, spun out crazy past return in junkie cabins in Topanga.

"It isn't good anymore, none of it." She spoke in a monotone. "I don't know why I left home. LA is hell." And: "When I get some money I'm going to buy a bar. You can make so much money running a bar. I want to run a gay bar. That's where the money is. That's where it is. Watered drinks at a dollar apiece."

"You'll never have any money," I said. "You're a loser, honey."

"Fuck you. You're so damn smart, you tell me what to do."

The following night after sex she was cold and her nose itched from the cocaine, and she lay wrapped in a blanket on the far side of the bed away from the air-conditioner, not wanting to leave, talking maniacally to justify remaining after sex without the pusher's excuse of having made the connection and thus bought the territory.

"You must have a lot of money. This is a nice room."

"I'm not paying for it."

"Like hell you ain't. You're a lousy aristocrat."

"I'm a radical."

She laughed. "Sure. And I'm the Queen of France."

The third night, she said, "I had two abortions. I thought I died each time."

"You should have gone to New York."

"There wasn't a New York then."

"There is now. It's free in New York. They suck you out with a vacuum."

"I couldn't take it again. I'm eighteen."

"You're a liar."

"I wish once I'd find somebody who'd stick by me. They're all on drugs."

That night she left my hotel room while I was asleep. She took my tape recorder and my portable typewriter. She wrote PIG on the bathroom mirror with her lipstick.

When I woke in the morning and saw the writing on the mirror and learned of the theft, I did not understand why she had done it. Even hustlers don't punch that low. Maybe she needed the money.

That afternoon I took a plane to San Francisco. Jann would be there.

15

Eller was nowhere to be found. I spent two days searching the hippie areas and Berkeley for him. No one in the movement had seen him in months.

I spent the evenings at the Minimum Daily Requirement, a coffeeshop in the North Beach district of San Francisco. Writers and heads and radicals and others with very little bread hung out there to pass the time. North Beach, like the city itself, was in its very tranquillity suspect. It was dated in sensibility, more fitted to the tame and self-conscious rebellion of the fifties than to this age. Regrettably, like so much that is charming, it was daily less germane to contemporary life. It had become a tourist attraction, admittedly one threatened by the burgeoning expansion of drugs and violence, threatened as everyone was by the symptoms of youthful sorrow and despair. So many of the young could not make life work.

Late one night I came into the MDR to join a friend of mine, Robert, who was a first-year graduate student at Berkeley. Robert was somewhere in his late twenties, wore a beard and a pair of wire-rimmed glasses, and he was fond of gossiping about Ginsberg and Ferlinghetti and other North Beach celebrities, speaking about them intimately as if he knew them personally when his talk was only bullshit and dreamstuff born of envy. Robert wanted to be a poet and discovered it was too hard a thing. He became a talker.

minimum
daily
requirement

We discussed writing and writers for a time, and then Robert asked me why I had never married.

"I don't think I've had the time."

"That couldn't be it."

"Maybe not. I get bored fast, you know? It's hard to make friends with women. Fucking is simple. But friendship? I never thought it would work, the two together."

"Smart man." Robert shook his head. "I never should've married the goddamn bitch."

"Why don't you leave her?"

"I have. Two months ago. I couldn't take the shit anymore. We had very little in common after a while. I guess you sensed that."

"No, I only saw you together a few times. Last time was in Chicago. I think you were with Abbie or going to see him or something."

"Yeah. Something like that. God, I don't know. She complained all the time about not having a goddamn life of her own. Balls! She had a fucking job and more friends than me. She was into women's lib. Once a week she and six girl friends took over the apartment. They'd lock me out. Literally lock the fucking door in my face. *I* paid the godramn rent. *My* fucking apartment. Finally she said she had never reached orgasm with me during our marriage. Not once. Do you believe that *gall*? We screwed every night, for Christ's sake. Now she is telling me it was *my* fault *she* didn't reach orgasm. That was *it*. The arrogance of that bitch! I told her to get the hell out. She wouldn't, so I left."

"Where's she now?"

"Living in Oakland with her sisters. That's what they call each other, *sisters*. I think they're a bunch of dykes."

"I don't think so."

Robert asked me what I was doing. I said not much.

"I read about that concert of yours."

"You mean in New York?"

"Were Mailer and Williams really there?"

"Yeah."

"Fantastic!"

"We lost money."

A girl Robert knew came into the restaurant and, uninvited, sat down at the table. He ignored her pointedly. Vicki, about eighteen years of age. Where Robert talked incessantly and smelled of sweat before you reached him, Vicki was squeaky clean and starched, like children in an orphanage on Visitor's Sunday, simply dressed, her hair shiny like a river.

I did not know whether it was her skin or the fineness of her face, but she reminded me of a girl I knew three summers before in Boston, Karen, who went through a police bust with me and had about her a vulnerability before life which attracted me. I made it with her once on the Common. After the bust I lost her, and hadn't seen her since. I wondered many times if she went back home—she was a runaway—or if she drifted like so many others into drugs or worse. I missed her, Vicki reminding me of her so strongly that I spent the night apologizing continuously for calling her Karen.

Robert talked with me about the situation on the Coast, the relative collapse of organized radical groups on campuses and a corresponding growth in aboveground electoral organization (Tom Hayden himself had become involved in city politics) and in underground actions, the bombing of police stations in the Bay area. We discussed the decline in the police vendetta against the Black Panthers and talked about Berkeley. I told him about the letter from Jann Eller.

"He's on a death trip," he said.

Events in the late sixties were the high points in Robert's life; he really felt like a hero marching in the streets in support of the People's Park, shoving daffodils into the barrels of the guardsmen's rifles, handing out pamphlets, later raging against the gas-bombing from the sky and the death of a comrade in the protest.

"It's a parking lot now," he said. "They put a big mother of a fence around it and poured shit over the flower beds and sand lots, and that was that. But nobody uses it, did you know that?" Hand on my arm, notice the triumph, "*No-body*! Never any place to park a car, and yet nobody will park in that fucking Regent's parking lot. God *damn*, that's beautiful, that people should remember."

A defeat was what I saw, a defeat delivered in the hard-headed pragmatic American way—asphalt—the symbols, green park and tar lot, deliriously appropriate to the values of the contenders. A defeat, and that was never beautiful.

"A great victory," I said sardonically. "A boy blinded. Another murdered by police fire. Hundreds injured without justifiable cause." Bitter that night, I was down and I needed a drink and only coffee and tea were to be had that late.

"What are you doing now, Robert?"

"Oh, I'm in school. You know that. And I work part time. Listen to this. At the Bank of America."

"Get out of here!" I laughed, it was too neat.

"Yeah, as a computer programmer. I cancel your checks."

Vicki was from Isla Vista, where a year or so before she had spent a few days traveling with the future and watching the Bank of America burn, watching the landlord offices and realty firms smashed by thousands of students making insurrection. (Those days in Santa Barbara were like a few other events in my experience—the siege of the Justice Department was another—where I was conscious of witnessing a rehearsal for revolution, simple, spontaneous flash-forwards in American experience, a revolution which never quite seemed to materialize.) Vicki was radicalized by the experience, the conversion complete inside before any corresponding change outside—she continued to dress like a daughter of Middle America.

We spoke about Santa Barbara and then moved on to drugs. I mentioned that I had some Percodan in my room, a drug that gave a nice high.

She came to my room with me. It was near Market. We took the narcotic. We lay on the bed and rambled about the violence we both confessed we dug. She felt scared about its attractiveness to her. We both lay on the bed, my hands over her body, fondling her hair as we absentmindedly spoke of bombings, dark crimson feats—government buildings blown apart like bursting balloons, the headquarters of corporations leveled, bank robberies to raise cash for actions, terrorist cadres—the infant romance of murder for a cause curiously appealing. Gossip of political assassination darkening the air. It was oddly restful to me, restful in that it played to hopes I had so recently abandoned in recognizing the futility in my own life of the engagement with political violence, the inability of the American left to pull itself together . . . so in talking thus I waxed nostalgic, falling verbally into a role that had once been true for me at Columbia and Washington and was true for me no more, and which I missed. We could have been discussing football or dishing movie stars, it was so easy, matter-of-fact, the content of the conversation unreal to me in the room with her with the weather warm and life comfortable for me that night, the confusion forgotten for a time; yet it was true that youths had died that year in awkward, self-defeating stabs at making revolution. Unreal. And to think that I had once believed revolution was coming, within two decades surely, believed it as I believed in my existence. In a sense, that hope had been my existence. It was no more.

It was difficult to accept the reality of Vicki in my room jabbering of "blowing the government to bits, into teeny pieces," difficult when I wanted to fuck and my head was compartmentalized to the degree that her talk was getting in the way of erection (*one thing at a time, baby, one thing at a time*) and she was eighteen and cold-steel words, bitterness, are unattractive in a girl that young; but it was more difficult to consider then what had happened to my certainty of revolution.

To get on with it: because of her middle-class dress and polite speech I had trouble seeing her as a "revolutionary," a word she liberally applied to herself. The words were militant; the *tonality* weakened the effect. I did not take her seriously. Male chauvinism.

"I hope it comes," she said, referring to the revolution if not to me. "I *know* it will, and the bastards'll get it up the ass!"

"*How* do you know?"

"I just do. I just do." It sounded unconvincing.

She took a shower and I got undressed and moved to join her in the tub under the water and she said, "Don't come in," and I stood in the bathroom on the mat working my meat and thinking of her in some butch cadre of women fighters battling the police like a man (the male shit again), working myself hard, and she pulled open the shower curtain and stood there a moment with her hair fallen like a canopy over her face, covering the hollows of her cheeks, one hand relaxed and shielding her sex with bourgeois demurement, like Venus Rising. "Hand me the towel, please," she said and laughed and shook the hair out of her eyes and moved her hand to brush it back, exposing her sex with the gesture, and then she was real to me because I remembered violence, like cold hands on my skin under a sheet.

In Washington, after the action at the Justice Department, I and thousands of other demonstrators tore through the streets into the commercial district of Washington, breaking windows, tear gas everywhere, and attempted to make a rush toward the White House, only to find Pennsylvania Avenue blocked by a wall of leather-crusted cops, the President's personal *Einsatzgruppen* portrayed in silhouette before a bank of bright searchlights gathered to blind us, and the rush dissipated and broke before the police and the gas. I went into an Episcopal church downtown. Everything was closed, the shopkeepers abandoning the city to the demonstrators and the police. My eyes were running and my throat dry and I wanted to wash. My shoulder had been clubbed and was badly bruised. In the church the nave was open to the protesters, youths scattered throughout the church, sleeping in pews, arguing, lighting up joints as the priest moved among them (a liberal: "God has no politics," when I asked him why). I went into the bathroom in the building off the nave and out in the hall were a half-dozen naked high-school boys, some shower-wet and drying themselves off with their clothes for lack of a towel, some with lesions on their bodies, their eyes bloodshot, tired and glistening. Inside, leaning over the basin washing my face, behind me the shower stall, I straightened up and with my eyes blurred fumbled around for a paper towel. There were none. A youth, younger than Vicki, was in the shower, a friend behind him under the water. They were singing "The Sinking of the Good *Reuben James*," shouting it lustfully off key, "Tell me what were their names, tell me what were their names. . . ." Seeing me groping for a towel, they stopped singing. The first boy reached down and lifted his shirt off his clothes piled on the floor and handed it to me. "Here, man. Use this." I took it and wiped my face. I turned around and looked at the boy, naked and *comely* (a biblical word, that is what he was), and he stared at me a moment, his hair plastered against his forehead dripping wet, his friend grinning at me from behind him in the stall. "Thanks," I said, and the boy flicked his head back and smiled, and as he did he moved his hand and brushed the wet hair away and exposed a deep gash on his forehead just below the hairline, that gesture seen before in Chicago with Eller in the shower and at Columbia with Dave Jones badly beaten dropping his towel as he wiped his hair off his forehead. He exposed a deep gash. His smile was one of pride, his badge of courage. Maybe he was seventeen.

And to understand the effect of that incident on me is to understand something of the sexual basis of violence and its relationship to establishing manhood, to the appeal of the scores of youths with whom I faced police violence over the years, whom I saw stomped and was unable to aid and whom I loved for both their absurd courage and the profitlessness of its waste. It is to understand why I could find it handsome when my friend Stephen used a penknife to please me . . . in Easthampton, the summer before, on codeine and grass, naked by a pool with several other stoned friends and Stephen asked, "Are you bored?" and I replied, "Dying of it." And Stephen, he was twenty-one, old enough to know better, said, "Watch, this is for you" and grabbed a knife and with its point cut the letter R into his thigh while I watched too stoned to move and oddly excited sexually by what I saw. Stephen smiling. The youth in Washington. That was how Vicki smiled at me in the shower, and remembering the youth in Washington I wanted her. This I knew: they were better than me, for they were immediately open to violence as they were open to life like a smooth beach open to the sea, without having to come to it as I did, step by step, having to think it through. That I envied, their apparent lack of guilt over the natural pleasure they took in violence.

16

Two days later I had run out of Percodan. I had also run out of patience with Vicki, quickly becoming irritated by her dependency and her rhetoric, which, once the initial sexual curiosity I felt for her had been satisfied, had come to sound shrill to me. She could not mention any political subject without my taking it as an indirect nag. I felt guilt over my political inactivity. No matter how often I told myself that speaking and writing would more than make up for the relative insignificance of my physical presence at demonstrations and my work in organizing, I still felt the itch of guilt. What I suspected was that in growing up somehow at last the balance between my physical cowardice and my will had shifted and I was now using the role of writer as cover for what was physical fear.

But that was too deep a subject for me to examine after several days on narcotics, so I slipped it to the back of my mind and headed for the airport, anxious to get to New York, thinking that once there I would work out my confusion over what I was now vis-à-vis writing and the movement.

New York. I spent an evening at the house of Joe Dallesandro, one of Warhol's superstars. Joe and Paul Morrissey and I watched a replay of a show on Andy Warhol I had hosted for educational television.

the
best

After the show the telephone rang and Tennessee Williams called asking us to meet him at Max's Kansas City, which was uptown from the East Village where Dallesandro lived.

Someone at Tennessee's table made a remark about Jim Morrison of the Doors dying in France. I had known that, but it had not struck me as a reality until the remark was made that night. And I think my response was indicative of my feelings about Morrison and, more important, about men.

Morrison died in a bathtub of a heart attack brought on by booze, or by booze and barbiturates, a combination I myself was familiar with. I had known Morrison slightly, and identified with him, and I thought his death was appropriate to him: Morrison lying naked in the tepid water, dead in the house where he had gone to write, his mind battered prematurely, like some beaten fighter's face, by whiskey and bad times and too much cheap exhibitionism before too many people for too little purpose. It was as a writer that I thought of him, trying to clean the brain cells in time, to make the words work for him in France. There was something heroic in that, even if it was a long way to go to make the writing break your way.

I was convinced Morrison knew it was over, the music, the rock style he represented, much as I was convinced that the movement as it had existed was over, finished before his dying. I thought of Morrison near the end, two years or more before when I had last seen him, his mind befogged, half stoned, in a haze, a stupor at once erotic and blind, through which the world's screeching and crackling came at him bent and terrible, like mad voices traveling on shortwave frequencies from far cities to his ears.

For days I could not free my mind of the thought of his death; not simply because he was among the first row of my generation to drop, it was more than that, more intimately related to my conception of manhood and the sense of identification I felt with him. So I pictured him lying naked and at rest, Morrison, who had played it out on stage in a sexual rage as controlled as it was violently beautiful, more whorish than manly, who in every gesture hurled contempt at his audiences, manipulated them, sent girls squealing wet-pantsed in the front rows of the Fillmore, and sent me into a panic of penis envy and confused threat before the face of that famous cock beneath the clinging black leather pants, thrust against the mike stand, rubbed by his hands. Morrison celebrated early death, certainly the death of old America. (*"Father, I want to kill you!"* and *"All the children are insane!"*) He was proud of the fact. So I considered him the best of my generation in this alone: he understood that unreason claimed our allegiance. His music insisted that love was sex and sex was death and therein lies salvation.

But I did not believe that Morrison understood sex. It was his enemy, an enemy he tried to become to defeat. It was death and unreason that Morrison was intimate with, that enticed him, enthralled and excited him. That is what made his act true for me, and what made him a brother of mine. I loved the tough guy because he was out hustling in the good fight, wrestling with the demon angels, fighting dirty. Good for him. He always grabbed for the balls. His music was aggressive, rugged, filled with raw images of death and violence overlaid with the juices of sex. *"What have they done to our fair sister? Ravaged and plundered and ripped her and bit her. Stuck her with knives in the side of the dawn, and tied her with fences and dragged her down."* Morrison celebrating the state of the world.

I considered his music and his lyrics to be like the writing of second-rate, dead-end punks aping Hemingway and not getting it right. Morrison, I thought, misunderstood manhood. But like me he was driven to try and seize the assurance of manhood which escaped him, and in the urge he blundered, confusing style with substance. That was Mor-

"When the Music's Over"—words by The Doors. © 1967 Doors Music Co. Used by permission of the author and publisher.

rison, all bluff, his class was that of a street hustler gone careening into impotence, raging and frightened before it, and working to pry the bills from the pig-john's fingers through rough tease and overpromise and funky, dazzling, crotchy foreplay. To grab the money and run before the fraud was discovered. Morrison was all foreplay. Nothing else.

The last time I saw him, when he was not performing on stage, was at the Bitter End coffeehouse in the Village. He was dressed in corduroy trousers, no underwear, a maroon wool shirt, and boots. He stood in the back next to me, and in the light from the stage where pop singer John Sebastian was performing, I could make out his long neck under the uplifted chin (*"I am the Lizard King!"*). But the handsome, fallen angel's face was bloated and sagged with fatigue under his high cheekbones, over his chin line, his eyes puffed and bloodshot and narrowed (it was always his wide eyes that betrayed the tough-guy, street-boy pose, that gave the lie to his public image), and his belly hung over his belt like the belly of any other worn-through Mick barfly. He was aging fast. Nearly my age, a few years on me, and I could see my future in Morrison, blurred, out of shape, the muscle tone gone in the swill of booze.

John Sebastian, the Erich Segal of rock, filled the Bitter End with cheap sentimentality, with Middle America's Rod McKuen romance, with weakness and Sunday-school images. Morrison stood against the wall listening, languid, unsmiling, swaying occasionally, like a professional boxer out of training watching amateurs sparring in the ring. Morrison's entire act was a practiced rage against the very falsehood in feeling, the sham, of John Sebastian's mentality which spread like goo over the room. Morrison no longer gave a damn.

"So when the music's over, when the music's over, when the music's over, turn out the lights, turn out the lights."

He is dead, I thought. He is gossip now. We are ending not in an explosion but in a flaccid slide (dead drunk in a tub). Ten years ago, let me repeat, ten years ago if anyone had told me I would live to see some of my friends, my contemporaries, dying at my age and younger, dead of booze and smack and impossible sex and defeat so massive it ends in seeking death, no, I would not have believed it. And yet they are dead, dying at my age and younger when I wish them still fucking like crazy on some goddamn beach, brown and sun-streaked, or rodding ape-shit souped-up along the Strip. That, too, is sentimental. I wish them life.

At Max's Kansas City I talked with Paul Morrissey, who had been with Jim Morrison on several occasions.

"What was he like at the end?"

"He was bewildered."

"Is that all?"

"He didn't know what he wanted. He went to Europe to be alone. It was too late then. He should have left three years before that."

I thought of Morrison freaked out and playing for the photographers (he hated the rock press) by hanging dangling at a distance beyond the camera's focus, swinging like a bell from a church steeple. Fuck the fucking world. Fuck you boppers and rockers and groupies and leeching chicks. Fuck you all. I thought of him Maced in New Haven. Of him in his birth state, Florida, finally giving up the pretense and admitting the actual nature of his appeal, ending the point of the tease. Showering contempt. *"Ya wanna see it?"* he shouts at the screaming groupies, dirty little girls with their feminine secrets and their cowardly, plain minds stuffed with simpering never-to-be realized sex dreams churning up their bowels. (But what have they? I suddenly grown sympathetic . . . clumsy groping fingers of adolescent boys under the fluorescent lights of McDonald's. How can you make a life on that?) *"Ya want it?"* the wet-pants jumping by the thousands in the Florida heat before the stage, tearing at the air. No elegance left. No style. *"Ya want it? How fucking bad?"* So Morrison says to hell with it, the act is finished, the whore's tease completed; he gives way at last and pulls it out from under the leather and gives the people what the people want. And later the people's police arrest him for indecent exposure, corrupting the morals of minors, etc., etc.

At Max's, Tennessee and I talked about male hustlers and then about death and Morrison's death was mentioned again. Williams asked all of us at the table, "What was he like?"

One of the boys, thinking the question meant, What was he like in bed? answered, "Just another Mick cock." He told a story about him, which no one believed. But I was angered by the lisping, self-dramatic implication that Morrison made it with boys, for that would be another betrayal, taking from my world one more supportive myth that someone of my generation having been tempted went through it with his sexuality tough, hard, intact, straight, unspoiled, uncon- fused. And yet for me the awful suspicion took root that Morrison was as busted up and bent as I, and his sexuality as tortured as my own. Still I saw him as a friend, and as a friend I mourned his dying.

"Baby," Tennessee said, "Don't be concerned. Death is awful. But it's *so* common."

"I pay it too much mind. It obsesses me."

Tennessee, smiling: "We somehow replace those who leave us. That's the wonder of it."

"I don't know, Tenn. I have never been able to figure out what it is, well, why I have known so many people who got into trouble so early. I got to stop this goddamn worrying about people. It's bad shit."

Tennessee ordered another round of drinks. And started singing.

17

Months later.

The war continued to prey on my mind. I felt totally powerless.

In April I wrote to a friend.

I spoke with Dave McReynolds of the War Resisters League and others in the movement by phone yesterday. I don't know what good I can do anymore.

How badly things go for Vietnam, for the people there, for the children in the villages. It is on my mind so heavily these days.

Yesterday in the Village in the afternoon on Sixth Avenue I spoke with a young Vietnam veteran. He sat in a wheelchair behind a table asking people to sign petitions against the war. There is no hope there.

The war cost him the use of his legs. At twenty-one, and yet he was filled with good humor and modesty, a sweetness to him. And I was ashamed again of my penchant for self-pity and self-indulgence. I was ashamed of my inactivity. But I can do little anymore. It is even difficult to write.

He had dark hair with blond highlights which glittered in the sunshine. His chair glittered also, the chrome catching the light.

I do not know why I am recounting this, except it increased my feelings of helplessness over the war,

spring-
falling

my guilt and grief in the face of it. When will it end?

Vietnam . . . I think of her now. And I have no words to describe my grief for her, outrage broken into grief, slowly grief becoming numb.

There are no words anymore.

The crimes against her have grown too large for language.

I think of Denise Levertov's poem about the people of Vietnam:

There is an echo yet, it is said,
Of their speech which was like a song.
It is reported their singing
resembled the flights of moths in moonlight.
Who can say? It is silent.

In April Richard called from Cornell and asked me if I would join in organizing an automobile train for the Vietnam Veterans Against the War to take from New York to Miami for the conventions.

I told him I hadn't the time. It would be the first major antiwar event I failed to participate in. I felt numb.

In May. On a Sunday.

I brought a friend of mine, Christopher Makos, to the hotel to join Tennessee. From there we took a taxi to the Isle of Capri restaurant for lunch. Tennessee had returned the day before from Minneapolis. I felt exhausted. Sex the night before. Brutal and rather cruel. I didn't know what was happening to me. My body hurt, my chest especially, my tits. There were bruises on my thighs, already yellow-blue in color like damaged melons. Dark circles under my eyes. I thought it was from the codeine. I was not sure. It was beginning to frighten me.

"Dotson takes too many pills," Christopher tattled. And

it came from his concern about me. Who did he know to appeal to who carried any influence with me but Tennessee? He was frightened of my habits. They were contagious, he thought.

"One needs them to work, the pressure." I glared at Christopher and went on with my explanation: "It's the price you have to pay to write."

"You haven't written in weeks, Dotson. You never work, that's why you're so broke all the time."

"I *do* work! Only I'm *selective* about it. All artists are selective!"

Christopher shook his head. He did not buy it.

"Dotson, do you drink when you work?" Tennessee asked me. "When I was your age, before I was thirty-five, that's when I started drinking when I'd work. Uhhh, the martini to get going, you know, later speed, and coffee, cups and cups and cups of coffee." (In Key West with Tennessee the winter before I would begin working each night about eleven. I would work until dawn when, at about five in the morning, I would come downstairs and make coffee in the kitchen before I went to sleep. Tennessee would be there, having just gotten up. We would have coffee each morning, talk for a time, and then he would make a martini and go off to his studio to write, taking what I had written that night with him. At lunch he would criticize what I had written and I would read what he had completed that morning. We were a relay team. We fed each other. It was good. For a time.)

"I usually have a drink before I begin. But I always drink endless cups of coffee," I said.

"That's because you're an alkie," Christopher interjected.

"Hell, I've *always* started with a drink. It's a habit of mine. Perfectly innocent. Why, even in college—"

Christopher again, tugging on Tennessee's sleeve: "*Dotson takes too many pills.*"

Tennessee reached over and touched Christopher's hand. "Baby, you mustn't worry. Dotson does what he has to do. We're *artists*. We are *compelled* to do what we must in order

to work. You have to survive, to make it through, at whatever cost." He smiled, and then turning to me, growing very
serious, "You will remember about burying me at sea?" He
asked the question intensely. It preyed on his mind, his
death.

"Yes, 'one day north of Havana.' "

"I wrote it in that book I gave you, Dotson, one day north
of Havana." He said it like a poem. "Back to the *sea*. I love
fishes. I am terrified of worms. Of being eaten by worms.
Rather the sea . . ."

Christopher: "That's where life began." Good boy.

"Yes, baby. It is going back, back to our origins . . . er,
like being recycled . . ."

"Like soda bottles." My gallows humor.

"Ha! Yes! Only newly *cleansed!* I am burnt out inside, a
burnt-out man . . ."

That comment of Tennessee's confused Christopher. He
became very concerned. "No, no you're not," he said. Tennessee was moved by his compassion.

"It's true, child. I have worn out my body, burned it up.
Worked it to death. I have said *life* to life, and I will say
death to *death!* I think of going to Italy. Maybe this week. I
can't go to Asia, not again, not now . . ."

"Why Italy? Jesus, it's falling apart." I did not want Tennessee to leave.

"In Italy . . . I can get a handsome gardener . . . a gentle
gardener . . . and raise goats and geese. I love goats and
geese. And a small garden with a view of the water."

"Oh, Lord."

"Yes, and you could come over, and Ruth, and you could
write there in my small house with its view of the water,
and we'll go into the village at night and watch the boys
and girls. I love Italians."

"But I thought you were going to Long Island." (Tennessee had told Christopher earlier that he might take a house
on the Island for the summer, which delighted Christopher
greatly, thinking of all those weekends on the beach.)

"Long Island's shit," I said. I hated the Island.

"I don't want it! What's out there? A lot of boring rich people. But Italy. . . ."

Christopher tried to make a case for a Long Island house, "In the Hamptons there are writers and artists and things. . . ."

Tennessee glared at him. "Three *hours* from *New York!* I'd die of *boredom.*"

Tennessee noticed Christopher was not eating.

"You got to eat, baby. You children don't take care of yourselves. You're only twenty-three, child, and to be so *worn.* . . ."

Tennessee glanced over at me, rolling his eyes. Then he asked Christopher, "What are you *on,* baby?"

"Nothing."

"We *know* you are on *something.* Hmmmm, you can tell *us.*" Tennessee looked over at me. "You kids want to die. Both of you. You don't love life. I have only a few years left, at most, at the outside—"

I cut him off. I was tired of the talk of death.

"Bullshit. You'll outlive us all." I laughed, patting him on the back.

"*You,* maybe." He was serious. I was suddenly very nervous. He stared at me, leaning forward, his arms resting on the table. "Maybe I'll outlive you. You aren't going to live to be my age, Dotson. You're too self-destructive. I *never* drank as hard as you at your age. I don't understand." He shrugged. It frightened me, his prediction.

"Eric Mann said we wouldn't go to the mountain, remember?" I replied. Eric had visited Tennessee and me the week before.

"I have gone, Dotson, many times." Tennessee shook his head from side to side, rolling his eyes upward. "I will go again. Only a few years left, you know. Hmmmm . . . and you *have* to *love* life with so little of it left to you."

"You said I was a survivor."

"I don't know, baby. I *thought* you were."

And then: "I want to have children, Tennessee. Very badly."

"Nothing's stopping you."

"How come you never had children? Don't you want children? I want them. I want a son very badly. Bad enough it hurts."

Tennessee looked at me a moment. He was offended. Then he smiled. He caressed Christopher's hair. "*These* are my children. You are my children. That's better. It's enough."

In July.

I met Dave Dellinger for drinks in Midtown. We went to Act I on the top of the old Times Building in Times Square. We sat at a back table. Dellinger was wearing a short-sleeved shirt, his shirt pocket filled with pencils. He had on brown corduroy trousers and his usual pair of broken-down brown suede Hush Puppies. He was sunburned from Miami. He had returned three days before from the Democratic Convention.

We embraced when we met, Dellinger laughing, rubbing my back with his arm around me in that intense yet shy gesture of his.

We ordered bloody marys. I asked Dave about Miami.

"We missed you there."

"I'm sorry. I . . ."

"It's all right. It was a success without you."

"But just barely!"

He laughed. "We had at least four thousand people altogether, but there was a lot of competitiveness. The Zippies. Real adventurers. Maybe provocateurs. And of course, the usual trouble with PL."

"I didn't think the encounter with McGovern was good. I talked with an ABC reporter. He said they came in like animals, smashed things at the Doral Hotel."

"I know. They were looking for trouble. They wanted it.

And people see that on television and think that's the anti-war movement, that those crazies are *us*. You know PL. What can we do? We spent our time organizing the kids in the street. Dotson, we had a wonderful relationship with the older people in Miami Beach. We talked with them, told them that inflation was because of the war. They're on fixed incomes. They all hate Nixon. For good cause."

Two bloody marys apiece. Then we walked up Broadway to the offices of a possible contributor. It was terribly hot outside. Panhandlers, winos asleep on the benches, in the doorways. It was degenerate, Times Square, so unlike the place which spun my heart like amphetamine when first I saw it, wooed me, enticed me, changed me a long time ago. It was older now, as was I, and it was cheap and blatant now, without style, its scuffed majesty gone, its lights burnt out, even its sense of danger become vulgar, unsubtle, petty, cowardly. It held no adventure for me anymore, Times Square.

"The whole town's falling apart," Dellinger said, as we walked uptown past the sex shows and the porno bookshops. "Nixon. The war. This should be a subsidized area, the theater district. And the city doesn't have enough money to paint the benches. All wasted in bombing Indochina." Dellinger related everything to the war. Everything.

He asked me if I was coming down to Miami for the Republican Convention. I told him what I saw of the Democratic Convention on television bored me, and I thought the Republican would be worse.

"What does that matter? We go because of the war."

"Sure."

"We need you. This is when it's important. We have to keep the war before the people. Only the people can force an end to the murder."

"I know, Dave."

He looked at me and laughed, throwing his head back. "Of course you do. I get into a regular hang-up giving out the advertisement for Miami. The Chamber of Commerce should pay me a promotional fee!"

I laughed.

He put his hand on my shoulder, smiling. "You have to be with your old man."

"You ain't old."

"I thought I was your father. I thought you thought of me as your father." It was true. I did. But his saying it surprised and flattered me.

"I do, Dave."

"Then you'll come."

I said nothing.

At the meeting with the possible contributor I got drunk. Dave was disappointed in me.

"Pull yourself together, Dotson. I'm getting worried about you."

"So am I," I said.

The following day, Barbara Webster of the Peoples Coalition called and told me that we were being sued by someone who had gotten hurt at the cathedral during the benefit.

"I thought their insurance covered liability."

"Apparently it doesn't," she said.

"Why would someone sue the movement who supported the movement? It makes no sense."

"I know. But then CBS is threatening suit over our unpaid bill. And so is *The New York Review of Books.*"

That surprised me. *The New York Review?* But they were left! "I thought we paid that bill." It was a bill for an ad we took advertising the benefit.

"We owe them seventy dollars. We only paid half of it. If we don't pay up they'll sue."

"That's sweet of them," I said. It was very disheartening.

In July.

Christopher came to my studio late, about 7:30 P.M. We

argued. He was disgusted with my drinking. He was dressed in white tennis shorts and a sheer white trunk shirt, cut low so that his nipples showed. He wore white loafers. Upon seeing him I reeled: days since I saw him last, and he stood there deeply tanned, his hair blonder, his body thinner, in white, and at once I was reminded of Jann Eller . . . he is there again, on the white mattress, I in a daze from drugs.

"Why do you stare at me like that?" Christopher asked. He was visibly uncomfortable.

I lied and said, "We are going to Peter Glenville's. He doesn't like you dressed like that, like you're in underwear. What restaurant can we go to with you dressed like that?"

"But we're eating at Peter's *house.*" He was correct. I had forgotten.

I offered him a drink. He declined. I made myself another one.

"I would like to be shot here." He placed his tanned hand on the white shirt over his belly. "The red blood on white. That's how I want to die."

"No," I said, the question suddenly becoming esthetic. "It has to be higher. In the chest. In the belly, a bullet would burst you open there, the guts would ooze. No, it must be in the chest, where the blood is bright red and clean."

I imagined him shot down, in his whites, on the ground, his hair spread as on a hospital pillow, his body sprawled awkwardly, the blood seeping beautifully in an oval, face-like stain across his chest, his beautiful face caught in astonishment as he died. Christopher believed he was immortal, forever young. The beautiful usually do, while beauty lasts.

Walking through Central Park to the East Side, smoking a joint, he talked again of dying violently. We argued. He said I had become uninteresting.

"You do *nothing.* Why don't you go to Miami? You seem so aimless. God, I don't care *what* you do, but do something. You know before, whenever you got out of jail, you always seemed happiest."

"Not anymore. I'm tired of being that happy."

At Peter Glenville's we ate in the sitting room. It was a beautiful house, very elegantly furnished, very opulent.

We discussed the Democratic Convention. I said I believed McGovern would win the election. No one agreed with me. Glenville asked if I was going to Miami to demonstrate against Nixon. I said no. He was surprised and, I thought, disappointed in me.

We talked about one of the security people at the cathedral benefit. He was on the front page of the *Times* with his disclosure of the United States breaking the Soviet Codes. I did not trust him. Rennie Davis said he was an honorable man. None of us could understand his motives for making the revelation about the codes, nor why he continued to use a false name (Winslow Peck). "Perhaps he is a government agent," I suggested. "So many of them are." And it struck me that I had fallen into discussing the movement as "they," rather than as "us."

We sat around an inlaid marble table. A single candle burned in a gold stick at its center, the flame reflected in the mirrors and on the gilding. Peter left the room for a moment. Christopher put his hand over the flame.

"Keep it there!" I exclaimed, suddenly excited. He held it there for a second, and then withdrew it abruptly.

"It's boring," he said.

"Coward." I put my hand over the flame. Terrible pain. I withdrew it. My palm blistered and turned bright red. "Coward," I hissed again. He took my hand and licked it.

In July.

I could no longer sleep at night. So I spent the nights drinking.

In July.

I had dinner with a friend. Later we went to his apartment. I took one Demerol tablet at dinner. At his apartment I took two more. I was beginning to sink.

A male hustler and his girl friend arrived. They took off their clothes. We went into the bedroom and lay on the double beds, the hustler with my friend on one, the girl and I on the other. She wanted to go down on me. I could not get an erection. I had no will. She played with my body. She smelled like a subway, rank.

I called Christopher and asked him to come and get me. He arrived and came into the bedroom. The girl tore his clothes off. She started going down on him. I grabbed her by her long hair and yanked her face away from him. He moved over to the other bed. The hustler grabbed him and pulled him onto the bed.

"Take your goddamn hands off him," I shouted, "He's my *friend*."

I picked up a boot off the floor and hurled it at the hustler's head. A perfect shot.

I grabbed a lamp. "If you touch him again, you mother, I'll break open your fucking head!"

He left Christopher alone.

The five of us went into the living room. We played music. I sat on the couch next to my friend, whose place it was. Christopher sat on the couch opposite me, the girl between him and the hustler.

"I'm going to give you a ring," she said to me. She kneeled down before me and took my big toe in her mouth and began biting in a circle around it. I could feel nothing because of the Demerol.

"Stop that," I said and kicked her head with my other foot.

"Bastard!" She fell away, leaving a bright red ring around my toe where her teeth had cut into the flesh.

"You fucking Communists!" she screamed. "I know all about you, you sonofabitch. You're a goddamn nigger-lover! They're fucking cowards, muggers, you sonsofbitches. They don't even have the balls to rob like men, for Christ's sake! They go in packs like animals, jumping old ladies and kids and cripples. Fucking goddamn animals. They ought to take every fucking nigger and line those muggers up against the goddamn wall. They should bomb them like they do those dirty commies in Vietnam, wipe the animals off the face of the earth!" She was tripping out on racism and Christopher was laughing, watching her gone crackers, and I sat there feeling nothing; the hustler played with his penis, with the two chancres on its tip; and my other friend stared at her as if he was witnessing some horrible kind of madness. And I? I should have shut her up, punched her even. But I was beyond that. I did not care anymore.

"In Brooklyn we know how to treat those fucking . . ."

I asked her to make me a martini. She went into the kitchen and returned with a martini and a knife.

"Here, darling, drink it up like a good boy." She glanced over at Christopher. He giggled.

Then she took the knife and began drawing it down my arm. I felt nothing. I sat watching the blade slide down toward my elbow. She cut me lightly. Christopher laughed. My other friend jumped up and slapped her across the face. "Gimme it! Gimme that knife! Are you all crazy? Get out of here! You're drug trash, all of you! How dare you do that to him? How dare you? Out! Get out!"

I went into the bedroom and fell asleep.

Two days later. I took one hundred milligrams of Demerol. I took the phone off the hook. I was lonely for something that had passed from me unnoticed until what? Too late.

I remembered the boy in the shower in Washington singing: "What were their names, tell me . . ."

CBS-FM was broadcasting bathetic rock-and-roll records from the late fifties. That was high-school time for me. Football practice on the lawns of the military school I attended. Making out along the Mississippi. Those trashy songs etched my growing up in America.

I realized suddenly why Stephen cut the letter R into his thigh. I had told him that once in prep school I had argued with another classmate, a cadet officer like me, and we had drawn our ceremonial swords on each other and he had stabbed me in my right thigh below my sex and ever since any pain in that area was erotic to me.

I thought of all the people I had known since high school, faces and bodies, and now they were gone off somewhere.

To sleep I poured a couple of shots of vodka. I stood at the window of my studio and looked out at the cupola on the apartment house across the street. It reminded me of a tower at the University of Chicago across from which I stayed in a frame house with the first movement people I ever met, members of the Student Peace Union. It was the summer of 1961.

I remembered how fulfilling knowing them was. They came to represent a community I desperately wanted to belong to. So there I was drinking myself to sleep and wondering where the community had gone. I could think of no substitute to fill its absence.

For all my talk of "alternatives," nothing I knew about Tennessee Williams or Yevtushenko or Eller or Dellinger or anyone else was of help to me. For the first time in my life I had no purpose in living it. All I experienced between the December benefit and the afternoon, months later, when I stood drink in hand staring out at the cupola opposite my window, all of it led to the conclusion that I was without purpose. I was an outsider again.

I was unable to write. I didn't know why. I decided to go to another town where nobody knew me and therefore nobody was around to ask me why I was not working. I decided I would not come back.

part four

LAFITTE
IN
EXILE

18

Several months after Paul Goodman's son died in a mountain-climbing accident I sat with Goodman in the living room of his Chelsea apartment in New York City. Earlier we had spent the evening out together, the two of us going to the General Theological Seminary, where he had read some of his new poetry to a small group of seminarians, perhaps eight students in all. (That was what he was proudest of, his poetry.) The poems he read were ones written about his son. He cried as he read them, unabashed by his tears, sitting slumped in the chair with his elbows resting on the crude folding table before him, a white handkerchief held over his face, sobbing. One of the poems he read was written "For A Young Widow," and it too was about his son, Matty.

Playing too happily
on the slippery mountainside
my only son fell down and died.
I taught him to talk honestly
and without stalling come across
but I could not teach him the cowardice
and hesitation necessary
to live a longer life unhappily. . . .
A young man is untrustworthy.
In the morning satisfied

on learning
of paul goodman's
death

he gets up from your bed
and in the evening he is dead.

Goodman and I sat on the floor, our backs braced against the living-room wall. Paul complained to me about American youth, many of the brightest of whom he considered undereducated, far too cynical of history and too ignorant of their countrymen. He saw tendencies toward violence in them, arising from what he believed was a deadly impatience in their lives. It disturbed him greatly.

He told me about speaking at a symposium at some college and of being interrupted by a group of students who subjected him to rude and, he thought, incoherent attacks against his conservative-anarchist politics. These were young men whose cultural consciousness he believed, quite accurately, had been created in part by the influence of his work: *Growing Up Absurd, Compulsory MisEducation, Empire City,* and so forth. He did not understand their hostility and was baffled and resentful. Why me? he asked. Is this the generation to which I gave such hope?

The rejection of youth wounded him, for as he freely admitted, he was a homosexual and was in great need of the attentions of the young. He viewed young men, especially loners and rebels, as his adopted sons. Clearly he was enthralled by them, drew himself to them boldly, sucking in his breath and putting as good a face as possible on what was, at its root, a paternal loneliness. He gave a fierce attention to the young, exchanging knowledge for companionship, thinking it was a good bargain all around. He was a lover and a teacher and if, near the end, the latter function nearly extinguished the former, the drive for physical contact with youth was still in him, the body hunger still keen. It was from that that he took his energy and his hope. And with his son dead he found himself beached and dry, without male progeny. He was cut off too soon.

Goodman was dressed in shabby trousers and an old shirt and cardigan sweater, the sweater turned inside out.

He was indifferent to clothes. He always looked older than he was, so physically unimpressive on first sight that one took him for a janitor or plumber, an impression I am sure he would have been proud of. He loved the doers of manual labor, loved them as he loved street boys, seeing something as yet unbought, uncorrupted in their knowledge-from-experience, their empiricism and practicality, in their good humor and intelligence as yet untwisted, as Hart Crane put it, by the love of things irreconcilable. He was a romantic, not of the age, for he saw nobility in modest intelligence, in simple work, in the bodies of youths without illusions about their sexuality, boys with enough compassion (and that seems native to the sons of the working poor), for older men, a need of them, men whose lives they see in wreckage and do not blink.

Later that night, drawing on his pipe, his body slouched old-man-like against the wall, his face deeply lined with fatigue and sorrow, he again commenced reading his poems about Matty. He had told me that I was in many ways like his son. At least for this purpose: in reading to me that night, in his lonesomeness for Matty, I stood as surrogate.

Anyway, once more he began to cry. For a moment I sat listening to his weeping, deep and hoarse as the growling of some ancient, fur-tattered predator whose leg was clamped in the jaws of a steel trap, growling shaken and incensed by the coming of death.

The windows of the apartment were open, the air blowing in, the noise of trucks rumbling in the distance on the West Side Highway.

I stood up and went to the window, leaving Goodman to compose himself. I leaned against the sill, completely at a loss for words of comfort, for I am embarrassed by deep sentiment in men, by male tears. I could not handle it.

There was quiet. I turned. Goodman smiled at me, shrugging humorously at his failure of control. "I'm old. It's too damn easy to cry."

"You'll cope all right," I said. "You'll make do," the last

line skimming on the edge of parody of his book's title, *Making Do.*

"Yes," he said, pushing his glasses to his forehead and rubbing his eyes with his hands. "I have gone through so many people whose absence I did not think I could survive. Now I survive my son. It's wrong, isn't it? It's unnatural."

During the first week of August 1972, I was in New Orleans, staying at the Prince Conti Hotel one block from Bourbon Street in the French Quarter. My room was painted black, with a large canopied bed with a blood-red spread and four pseudo-Oriental posters with gilded dragons coiled around their crowns. Above was a skylight covered by a black slip which I could draw by pulling a cord . . . and that was pleasant, to wake in the afternoon and pull a cord and have the sky slide into view, pouring in sunlight.

I was in New Orleans because it is the best drinking town in the country, and one could go there broke (which I was) and live on credit cards and wake late in the afternoon and spend the hours until the following morning in the twenty-four-hour saloons, or in the humid streets crowded with Southern youths and their girls, witless and desperate with that sullen yet curiously optimistic, slow, indeed slovenly, drawling mentality of Southern street kids. Whether from Shreveport or Jackson or Panama City, Florida, they are poor white runaways from the backwaters, dropouts from junior and senior high schools. They were Paul Goodman's special concern and, for a while, mine. By the time they reach Bourbon or Dauphine or Burgundy Street they are hooked on the All-American Hustle, the ability with nighttime eyes to spot tourists under the commercial lights, easy lays, the lonely, the fed-up middle-aged, and once making the hit to turn the trick with natural although practiced charm, to you-all them into bed or strip their pockets in bars, to clean them of cash and credit.

Paul Goodman once suggested that prostitution be legalized, moreover encouraged, among teen-age boys, for it was, as he saw it, useful work. Well, there are rules to the boy-girl hustle that the Southern kid accepts and respects. They play the game with less class but more humanity than their peers in Chicago or New York. Maybe the lack of cold weather frees them from the terror that drives their Northern counterparts early into petty theft and scag and speed and the nodding death. I do not know.

What I do know is that these kids see the failure of older people, men of Goodman's generation, and respond to it decently. And that is to their credit.

I was in New Orleans because I had a book to write, due in November, that I did not know how to write. Or because I had written a play that was a failure. Or because the wars and the accumulated troubles of a decade or more seemed insoluble, and I felt powerless, defeated before it. Or because too many friends had gone off or been done in and had not been replaced, and I found the sheer arithmetic of life counting off against me. And, yes, this was it, because panic was exploding in the core of my brain. Work! and I could not work. Write! and I was devoid of language. Sleep! and I walked the streets in search of what, if not sleep? Beat the meat, drink, drink, Seconals and Nembutals in New York, the consciousness of life passing me. (I was only thirty, and my attitude even to me seemed prematurely self-dramatic . . . and yet it must be admitted that I watched my friends begin to break so soon, the tendons ripping, marriages split early in divorce, friends into drugs and alcoholism, into prison, several now into suicide, lost.) And there, near my toes, or rather under them where the nerves tingle when one walks on a hot beach, I felt the tendrils of future sorrow touching my feet. Paul Goodman had a favorite word for it: *anomie.*

Anomie, my ass. What is it when a writer cannot work and is overwhelmed by his own self-pity, and reaches thirty years and is given a birthday party by his best friend and his response, this writer's response, was to react like a sullen adolescent stoned on Boone's apple wine when he asked Mick Jagger, "Don't you know I'm thirty? Jesus H.! *Thirty! It's the slimy pits!*" And Jagger, his face gray, homely, unexceptional, yet awakened by amusement at this writer's drunken melancholy, smiles. "Man, listen, at thirty, that's when the bloody sun begins to shine!" Jagger was twenty-nine.

So the following day I climbed aboard a plane and headed for New Orleans, thinking I would never come back, or stay at least to drink it through, to hear, maybe once in my life, that click Brick keeps telling Big Daddy he waits to hear. Click! On the plane I thought about mortality and asked myself why I avoided politics and drank like a fish and was terrified each night unable to sleep, and why sex for me had grown violent, for I could only find beauty, well, satisfaction anyway, in its pain? Why the panic in the drunken, late-night phone calls to sleepy, irritated friends? Why did I live the life so badly? Ah, I thought, because I have no son.

The afternoon I left New York, I asked a friend to lunch. He was from New Orleans, where he maintained a house. We were both hung over from my birthday party the night before. I asked him to give me the names of some bars in the French Quarter. "Good drinking bars, none of this fag stuff."

"Defeats In Exile," he mumbled into his wine, answering my question. "That's a good bar. It's open all night, baby."

Open all night! Bingo! "Lovely name," I said, the romantic in me breaking forth in the redundant pity of that name, *both* the defeated and the exiled. "But what does it mean, where does the name come from, Defeats In Exile?"

My friend looked up at me, shaking his head. "No, no, baby. Not *Defeats* . . . it's *Lafitte In Exile*. The pirate, you know, baby? The pirate Lafitte. It has a fountain by the door with a flame burning in the center of it. Fire *and* water, baby."

"Yeah. Blood and sperm." I quoted Rimbaud, playing to my friend's Verlaine.

"Uhhh . . . it's a good bar, you know. The sailor bars are gone. That's where I used to drink. Now . . . hmmmm, now when I'm in the Quarter I drink at home. The Quarter, you know, it's all gone down . . ."

New Orleans, 2:00 A.M. Outside the bar Lafitte In Exile. I'd been drinking since three in the afternoon. I was feeling good, high but not drunk, given to giggling and open to provocation. The night before I had bought a whore (thirty dollars) in front of the Chateau LeMoyne, bought her drinks, and taken her back to my room where she lay on the bed stewed, her navy-blue panty-hose dangling like a warning flag from one ankle. She lay back and stared at the canopy, smoking a cigarette and, in a thick Delta accent, rattled on intensely about her old man beating on her in Baton Rouge and stealing her relief checks. Apologies, bad sex, more drinks, finally sleep. But now it was two the following morning. I left Lafitte In Exile and walked down Bourbon Street into the dark end of it toward the black district. Young hustlers and a few whores paced slowly, some cooing as I passed. A wino out cold in a doorway. I carried a drink in my hand. It was very hot, maybe ninety degrees. I enjoyed the heat, sweating.

"Give me some of that stuff." A young man sat on the stoop under a rusted iron gallery tilting precariously toward the street. I guessed the kid was about sixteen years old, maybe less.

"Sure. Why not?" I handed him the vodka.

He took a sip and spit it out. "What's that shit? That ain't bourbon."

"Vodka."

"Tastes like piss, man." He grinned, flirtatious. "You drink that poison?"

"All the time. What the hell do you drink, straight soda?"

"Bourbon and Coke. Bourbon and Coke."

He stood up. This is how he looked: about five feet nine, he wore dirty brown corduroy trousers with large buckle pockets on the front and the back, a pair of Frye stomping boots, a blue T-shirt. He had acne on his face, large blue eyes similar in color and depth to Jann Eller's, high cheekbones, his face gaunt and hungry. In a word, a schoolboy. His long hair was dyed orange-red with blond roots, like the hair color of black hookers on Manhattan's Eighth Avenue. The hair was dyed because he thought it made him look older, and when you are sixteen and preoccupied with hustling money and avoiding the vice squad, with getting into bars, it is important to look at least eighteen.

An hour later he and I were sitting in the courtyard of Dirty Pierre's Bar having breakfast. The kid was starved, and the writer, who was paying, sat in wonderment over the kid's dialect, his idiom and syntax, the intimate, familiar way he bent the language unself-consciously to his own devices. He spoke with the regionalism of Derek in Baltimore, and while they were separated by a thousand miles or more of plain and forest and history, they both were touched indelibly by the language of the hills, the bleak poverty compensated by the richness of their American speech. Paul Goodman loved this kind of boy, brash, naturally bright, pugnacious, speaking *un*-Standard English and at home in his body and his natural world. And this: free of the conceits and dishonesty of formal book learning, an exercise Goodman profoundly distrusted. I had seen Goodman on occasion grow excited in the presence of similar boys, Puerto Ricans in most circumstances, listening to them with a sympathy and patience he gave to few other people. Because he admired their strong capacity to make do, to survive.

I asked the kid where he was from.

"I'm from Arkansas. They call me 'Arkansas' 'cause my folks plant there. We all come from the Ozarks."

"What town?" If they were planters they were truck farmers at best, scratching out a subsistence. The hills there are poor and burnt out.

"Huh?" His mouth was full of food.

"What town are you from?"

"Ummmm, Camden. Hear of that? Camden, Arkansas? You ain't been there? 'Bout a thousand people, I guess. Naw, hell, I'm lyin'. Maybe nine hundred thereabout. What's this thing?" He held up an olive on the end of a toothpick, showing me with obvious disgust what he had discovered on his plate.

"That's a black olive."

"A what? That ain't no olive, them's *green*. What you want, huh? You after some boodie?" Suddenly suspicious.

I thought "boodie" meant loot. I said no.

"You ain't gettin' none. No how. I run away when I's fourteen. On the road, and this old man drives up and says, 'I give you ten dollahs to suck your pecker.' *Ten dollahs!* Man's crazy! Then I go to Shreveport. Trashy town, Shreveport. Houston. Mobile. Biloxi. Now here."

"Why do you stay here?"

He looked at me as if I were demented. "Why do you think, huh? Ain't got noplace else to go."

"Go home," I said. It seemed simple enough.

"Old man dead. . . ."

"I'm sorry. I really am."

"No shit, the old sonofabitch got hisself cut over. . . ." He ran his finger across his throat to illustrate. "Nigger done it."

All the while he spoke he shoved biscuits and runny eggs and home fries and bacon into his mouth as if he had not eaten in days (he hadn't), talking of missing ham jowls and grits and easy sex in the morning with the Baptist girls of Camden, Arkansas. And under it all I think the kid, Arkansas, was scared and working hard to keep this New Yorker's interest, maybe building it into some kind of working affection to take him beyond this one paid meal on to others . . . working, hinting, teasing, finally asking for a place to stay the night.

"My back's 'bout broke from sleeping on them streets. Shit, this ain't no fit way for nobody to live!" Then narrowing his eyes, "Man, I don't give boodie to nobody, you hear?" I nodded. "I ain't no nigger. Why I got to live like one of them niggers when I ain't one?"

I stood up and went to the men's room. When I returned to the courtyard I stopped at the bar before going to the table to rejoin Arkansas. I asked the barman to deliver another round of drinks. There on the bar was a copy of the New Orleans *Times-Picayune*. In it a short paragraph telling of the death of Paul Goodman in New Hampshire of a heart attack. He was sixty years old. He was gardening when death came.

I returned to the table shaken.

"What's wrong?" Arkansas asked. "You look heartbroke." It was asked sincerely, his hand reaching across the table and touching mine tentatively, shyly.

"It's nothing. Where's my drink?" I couldn't take in the fact of his death. It was unreal.

I called the waiter and asked him to hurry with the booze. I did not want to talk anymore. All I thought of was Paul Goodman alone up there on the farm when it came for him. I thought of the last time with him, of the bitter edge to our words. It was an unhappy moment.

"Hey, what's wrong, man? Come on!" Arkansas shook my arm.

"My friend died."

"What?"

"My friend. Paul was his name. He died."

"When?" He was already indifferent.

"Yesterday. In New Hampshire."

"What's that?" He did not catch the name.

"New Hampshire. That's a state."

"Shit, man. I knows that. There's fifty-two of them."

"No, just fifty."

"Hell, what you think, I ain't dumb. Fifty-*two!* Alaska and Hawaii." Of course.

I gave up. "Okay. So what? He's dead anyway."

Arkansas grinned, a little maliciously. "Hell, easy come, easy go."

Later, at the hotel. The skylight covered with its black slip to keep out the morning. I lay on the bed. I told the kid to take a shower.

"I don't need no damn shower."

"Like hell you don't. Arkansas, you stink real bad."

He grumbled and headed for the bathroom, leaving his clothes scattered across the floor, the clothes filthy, giving the room an acrid odor.

I lay on the right side of the double bed. Arkansas came out of the shower dripping water on the carpet as he walked to the bed, flicking his head back and with his left hand brushing the hair out of his eyes. He lay on the bed, his back propped against the headboard. He lit a cigarette.

"Wait a minute," I said. "Your hair's all wet. You're getting the damn bed wet."

"It ain't wet," and then he pulled up the spread and ruffled it towel-like over his head. "That okay now?" Petulant.

"Sure," I said. And then I noticed his arm under the light as he reached for his cigarette. "Let me see." I grabbed his arm. Track marks.

"Ain't what you think! Ain't shit, just speed!"

"You *shoot speed*?" I was worried for him, remembering how my friend Stephen died with a paralyzed heart the first time he shot amphetamine into his veins.

"Ain't really speed." He went over to his clothes and pulled a handful of vials out of his trouser pocket. He threw one to me. Demerol, an old friend.

He got back on the bed. He spoke a bit about his past, the dirt poverty, too many brothers and sisters, too much illiterate despair known too long. No wonder he was a beatdown angelic looking to be stoned. I listened to him with great sympathy as I have listened to other boys, thinking it was their complaint that originally drew me into activism and later into writing. It was their complaint, and the experience in America it represented, which I empathized with and in a perverse way envied. I thought how much better Goodman would have been with this boy, what he could have taught him, given him, when I had nothing, no advice, no more community of dissent, no wise counsel, just some overcharged credit cards.

He changed the subject. "Look at that." He touched his penis, causing it to grow erect, grinning at it like some half-wit saint before a miracle. "Ain't no fourteen inches, but it's a *good* pecker."

"Go to sleep, Arkansas."

"What you got me here for? Huh? Ain't goin' to get no boodie." I didn't know whether that was a question or a statement of fact.

"No *what?*"

"*Boodie*, man! *Ass!*"

"Go to sleep." I had no interest in his boodie.

He slept. I sat up on the bed, the lights out, and smoked cigarettes and occasionally reached for the vodka on the bureau. It was good not to be alone. I thought of Paul, of meeting him one afternoon at Rockefeller University in Manhattan where he was to address a conference on the relationship between science and government.

Goodman and I met in the vestibule of the auditorium. He approached me and asked if I knew when he was to speak. I said no. "Come with me then," and he took my hand and led me to the back of the auditorium and sat me down beside him on the red-carpeted floor. We waited there for his turn to speak. That is, we waited with Goodman holding my hand tightly in his, touching me on my thighs and stomach, whispering to me of his nervousness. I did not know then of the death of his son.

Finally he got up to speak. When he had finished he came over to me and said, "Please come tonight to General Seminary. I am reading my poetry there." He squeezed my hand and kissed me. I obliged him, for he asked with such gentleness.

We went outside. I walked him to the subway. On the way we passed a blond kid on the street and Goodman said he looked like a boy he knew in Chelsea. "He was on drugs for a while, Irish boy. Now he's off them." He paused. "Strong kid. I think he could break wine bottles between his thighs." He grinned, amused at the image.

Why I tell you here of that first meeting and his gentleness toward me and why, earlier, I spoke of his reading his poems about his son, is that I am convinced that he was broken irreparably by his son's death, that it cost him more than he could pay.

I think that because it serves to explain, in a kind way, his relationship to me. I can remember lunches in his apartment where he would cook me eggs and dump a tin of tuna fish on my plate and tell me to eat and then dive into speaking of what was on his mind. And it was usually an analysis, never completed, of his relationship to youth, of whether his work (his life) would survive. Fame came so late to him, so reluctantly, that he was never convinced of its permanence. He cared deeply that his work was read by my generation, and the criticism of some young people disturbed him enormously. He had been poor and relatively unknown for a long time, and if we—my generation and those younger, to whom he looked with such hope—did not regard him well, then what was it worth, what future was there in it?

What did he see in me? I was a young writer, emphasis on the adjective. He felt competitive with older writers, especially those whose work he considered lesser than his own but whose fame was greater. I was young enough for him to sustain a student-teacher relationship, however briefly, one free of envy. He needed to talk about his craft, his writing, with someone young. He made do with me for a time.

What finished our relationship, or rather put it in suspension, was his shy yet insistent physical demands. I do not mean that we ever had sex, but there was always sexual tension there, as there was between Paul and every young man to whom he was attracted.

One afternoon he took me into his consultation room, a small bedroom where he had a desk and a day bed. I lay down on the bed. He asked me to remove my shirt. He spoke to me so softly about my relationship with my parents (hostile) and my sisters (latently incestuous), about latent and unacknowledged homosexuality (a drum he never ceased beating), about the tension and aggression he believed I kept bound up inside of me, knotted there, breaking forth occasionally into violence.

"You don't know how to breathe correctly. Now breathe deep, no, no, with your *stomach, deep* . . . that's right, yes, let it out, let it out. No, no, not all at once. Slowly, like this . . . *whooosh* . . . *choooossh* . . . slowly, between the teeth, make a noise. Do it again, that's right, no, here," hitting my belly with his hands, kneading it like dough. "Fill it *up!* All the way! Fill it up, the chest, the lungs, now you've got it . . ." Hands on my chest, pressing in.

We had two sessions like that. Then he told me I needed therapy. I told him I could not afford it. He laughed. "Go into therapy with me." He was a Gestalt lay analyst. "I won't charge you. Well, not at first." Then, catching my skepticism, "Yes, later I will, something modest, something you can afford. It's part of the *treatment.*" He laughed.

It ended in my refusal to go into therapy with him. Partially because his presence was so intimidating and his need of what? affection? a son? so great that I feared that I would lose what independence and manly competence I had won if I underwent analysis with him. He was extraordinarily captivating, Goodman. He made you lonesome.

The last time I saw Paul was in the Village. He had read my novel, *Government Inspected Meat,* which had been published several months before.

"Did you buy it?" I asked.

"Buy it? I stood in the aisle at the Eighth Street Bookstore for two hours and read it there. You don't need the royalties."

He was disappointed by the book and spoke to me bitterly about it. "It's too antihomosexual for me, even antisexual. And you show too little respect for words in it. You hurl them at the reader. You commit assault with them. You're too young to be so angry, so violent." We argued. Seeing him —this was shortly before he left for Hawaii to teach at the university there—I realized how much I would miss him.

"Don't leave New York, Paul. It's stupid to make the move. There's nothing in Hawaii but beachboys and those goddamn rich scions of the missionaries, you know, the guys with the pineapple plantations and the defense contracts? The *life* is here in the city."

He scratched his head. "You're wrong, Dotson. The life's where you make it. This city's dying."

"No."

"Yeah. Yeah, it is. Look at its politics. Look at the left here. Look at its streets. Don't make fun of beachboys. They have a direct relationship with the elemental. They are modest because of it."

It occurred to me that it was that relationship he loved in his son and which he could not find in me. He had written of his son, "Probably the worst that can befall/is past me now, Matty being dead./If he were here he would have hoed/this field where my shoulders fail. . . ."

In New Orleans I felt emptied by the news of his death, drained, somewhat abandoned and resentful because of it, as if my errant father had died cheaply for no purpose, like Arkansas's old man in some pointless bar fight. But it was not cheaply. It was in working the earth with his hands, hoeing the field, in that "direct relationship with the elemental" that death came for Paul Goodman, Greenwich Village born, so completely urban in character that even his walk and carriage spoke litanies of the street. He ended on a farm. Hell, he was gone and I had moved up one place closer to the front of the line. And I had no son.

It was worse for Goodman. He had a son and lost him. I think that part of what made his homosexuality at the end so infinitely piteous is that it was charged not by lust (that we can understand and satisfy) but by the memory of a son who died one day absurdly. There is no help for that.

Why have I written all this? I sit at a table in the courtyard of Pat O'Brien's Bar in New Orleans. It is very hot. Fans blow, shuffling the paper on the table.

I see birds in the huge, ornate cage across the courtyard, a brown lizard surreptitiously slinking up the side of the cage, drawn by the flies drawn by the bird droppings—as I am drawn by . . . what, to this city? Sitting in the heat, slightly stoned on vodka . . . not leaving New Orleans I have left it already, as surely as Paul has left us and I have left what bound me politically to the past. Already, too late God knows, I have left Arkansas, who sits beside me here playing eager recipient to my young but not too generous role of Sugar Daddy. Paul, I do not play it well.

Arkansas sits here beside me in a pair of blue trousers I bought him this afternoon, trousers that Paul would appreciate, for they provide the kid with a basket that settles there between his thighs, thighs that will never crack wine bottles between their sinews, neither wine bottles nor this New Yorker's affections. They are too naïve for that.

He sits beside me as he sat days ago on Bourbon Street when Paul was alive at two in the morning, as I staggered out of Lafitte In Exile, drink in hand. He sat there on Bourbon hustling with a style Goodman appreciated but one that went out in the thirties or before, went out whenever it was Hart Crane last stumbled down similar streets.

What Arkansas represents is, I think, what Goodman and

I and others on the left saw residing in similar youths which touched our concern and made us see them as adopted brothers and sons—it is America done over and lost. One hears it in their accents, in their languid, untrained speech, in the tough swagger that disguises a pathetic vulnerability. They are trained for nothing. They have no place.

I, too, like Goodman, am an involuntary romantic, ashamed of sentiment. But it is America at bay there just the same. For that is what I met, and what Goodman forever sought to meet, that morning at two on Bourbon Street: the relic of an America murdered before my birth in Goodman's early years in the cells of the brains of his generation, most of whom (he expected) grew old and comfortable in their complicity in state and corporate crime, the men of rank and the terrace who spent from my generation's number its best in foolish wars.

"Matty," Goodman said. "If he were alive he would be in jail." That is crime enough.

I am moved here by the knowledge of leaving New Orleans and by the future memory of Arkansas, like the memory of Goodman's son, asleep in bed in the morning with his body prone on its side like the remains of some son lost. And I know he has no future and no past, no one like Paul to instruct him (I am not equipped for it), and that he is relegated within a handful of years to death by violence or drugs. There is no help for it. Looking at him, I see what Goodman saw and loved, I see what drew me into activism: all the youths who have no place in postindustrial America.

And who is to speak for them? Who is to worry about them now that Paul is gone?

last chapter:

Several weeks after I returned to New York from New Orleans, a startling thing happened. I began to bleed.

That is . . . by the time I came back to New York I had abandoned the attempt to write the book I was contracted for and simultaneously had almost totally withdrawn from any activity on the left, certainly from direct involvement in the antiwar movement. It was not that after so many years I had grown indifferent to the war. I was still sensitive to the conflict, outraged (although that word conveys levels of feelings that were beyond me now) by its continuance and horror; what had developed in me was the blunting of passion by the sheer knowledge of my own powerlessness to affect the war and by the realization of what nearly a decade of resistance to that war and to other injustices, what life on the outside in the streets and underground in the United States, had cost my friends. By the derangement of my personal life, my feelings about myself.

Let me illustrate. A friend of mine, a homosexual, lost his male lover to suicide early this winter. The dead lover was twenty-two. My friend's response to that death was withdrawal from contact with other people because feelings, affection, had suddenly become dangerous for him. Stripped of what he loved, torn from him suddenly, he was immediately open to anything. He was open to suicide himself, and to protect himself he withdrew. He kept to himself until he was able to heal inside.

home
free

Thus for me, by 1972, the question of survival had become very personal . . . as if death in Vietnam had infected my life with anomie, had lodged inside me. The question became one of my own survival. I had lost no lover to suicide. Instead I had experienced a series of defeats whose sum effect on me was equal to a loss as dramatic as my friend's. Only it was less specific.

Either because I was weak or because I badly wanted to survive, I was drinking too much, more than ever before in my life, and at the same time using drugs: Demerol, Phenaphen (old standbys), Quaalude (which I consider dangerous), and cocaine (a waste of money). Objectively it is a bad thing to use drugs, especially in conjunction with liquor. It is unhealthy. However, sometimes it is more dangerous not to, sometimes liquor and drugs are necessary to take you through, to make you live or to permit you to live when in a manner new and frightening and somewhat stupefying (because you cannot lay hold of its *immediate* cause) you discover that the will to die is housed inside your body and you are stuck with it, drawn to it by . . . what? Wide grief, fatigue, inability to handle stress, remorse? I do not know. You are ready to throw in the towel and you know you are looking for the excuse. Drugs help you avoid doing it.

That is not quite accurate. Suicide, to give it its name, takes courage and a degree of solipsism and insensitivity sufficient to end your life without too much concern over that act's consequences for the people you love. When you die by your own hand, you dump your life on your friends, you leave them hanging with it, baffled and guilty over it. You make them responsible, complicit in your life, in a way that living never did. And that is unfair.

I knew that I badly needed to write and could not bring myself to do it. And I found myself attracted to people and situations that were perilous for me in that they encouraged whatever self-destructive impulses lay inside me and they mocked or cheapened what was finally of value to me: writing and a commitment to the left, or to the victims in whose name the left moved. And the more depressed and remote I became, the more alarmed my close friends were. Perhaps I desired that response.

Late one night I had dinner with Peter Glenville and a young actor. Glenville, a close friend, was worried about me, and I was flattered by his evident concern. The night before this, I had been up until dawn drinking and then later, with a girl, hitting the juice bars. She walked out on me about six that morning, and in the leaving made some painful remarks about my standing as a man and a writer. I tried to shrug them off.

Glenville, the actor, and I were at the Buffalo Roadhouse, off Sheridan Square. I was drunk, which was expected by then. Someone called my name, and I got up and walked to another table at the far end of the bar, where a young man who had worked on the benefit at the cathedral a year or more ago sat having supper with his girl friend.

I stood a moment talking to him, leaning on the table to support myself. I noticed the strangest expression come across his face, a mixture of shock, bafflement, and displeasure. He stared at me oddly and then glanced down at his plate. I followed his eyes down, leaning on my hands over the table, and was equally baffled because blood seemed to be dripping rather heavily on his sesame hamburger bun. I couldn't figure it out.

"Your nose is bleeding," he said.

I wiped my nose and, sure enough, the dike had broken and blood was spilling from my nose. I took a napkin from his table, pressed it against my face, apologized, and returned to my table.

Glenville was upset over the condition of my nose, in part because blood had poured on my shirt front, and before explanations were made, it appeared as if I had at long last met the assassin's bullet. Ice packs were applied. The bleeding stopped.

The following night, during sex, I looked down to see the same expression of shock, bafflement, and displeasure which quickly soured into resentment as my blood fell on someone else's stomach. This time it took longer for the bleeding to stop. "It must be the cocaine," I said. "The insides of my nose are rotted out." It did no good, sex ruined, the damage done. You win a few, you lose a few.

What followed was a week of not leaving my studio, of waking in the early mornings or late at night terrified that I was suffocating from the blood running into my throat, waking to find the pillows and bed sheets covered with blood flowing from my nose.

I refused to change the bed linen. I was fascinated now by the look of it. It was like an Army field hospital or a hotel bed requisitioned by a revolutionary force during days of siege. That is how my mind works, melodramatically. It was ridiculous and yet oddly pleasing that I, who had so yearned for a dramatic, bloody, historical, public confrontation on the barricades, was dying of a nosebleed (so I thought) on Bloomingdale sheets in a studio overlooking Central Park. It was something out of Neil Simon.

And here I must tell you something I have avoided telling you but which you should know. When I was nineteen years old, in the fall, I attempted suicide in Milwaukee, where I was then living, in a tacky furnished room off Wisconsin Avenue. I spent a week or so locked in my room, not answering the telephone, letting my mind drift until I reached a state of indifference and unreality and boredom so acute that I began playing with my body as with a toy. About three in the morning I took a razor blade and slashed my wrists, and then held up my arms and, with the spurting blood as paint, drew pictures on the wall. It is an unattractive story, but a true one. (I had been reading Rimbaud and Huysmann, which says a lot.) A few minutes later I went outside, my arms wrapped in torn strips of bed sheets, and decided to walk to the hospital, which was about twenty blocks distant.

I collapsed on the street. I was arrested—attempted suicide was a crime in Wisconsin—and committed to Milwaukee County Hospital for observation.

I recall that here because I am aware of what in me triggers the series of events that lead to suicide. And if my enforced isolation, growing indifference to outside actuality, refusal to answer the phone, and finally, boredom were not symptoms enough, then the recurrence of an old dream, one I had repeatedly when I first tried killing myself, made the extremity of the situation unmistakable. I dreamed I was on the roof of a tall apartment building, on a pogo stick, bouncing on the stick along the edge of the roof while a large crowd of people, usually sailors, mingled below shouting up at me to jump over the edge.

I think what may have set this off was the fact that what was outside was wounding to me, intensely painful. I felt no place, or could think of nothing effective to do, within the movement. People I loved, young and full of promise, had died or gone off somewhere. Sex was bad and becoming inoperable. I was unable to keep my drinking under reasonable control. And I was lonely, not for anyone in particular . . . lonely in that I felt empty, like a tidal basin suddenly drained of water and lost without the weight of that liquid body, drained. I could conjure up nothing to fill the space inside myself created by the passing of so much. I felt like a lover haunting a city evacuated in a siege where every street corner held the remembrance of things once known and good and now gone. That too is romantic and maybe, in looking back, too easy a sentiment. But that is how I felt.

The bleeding . . . I discovered that if I masturbated my nose would bleed, sexual tension raising the blood pressure, and immediately after orgasm a rush of blood would come. Which seemed to me an oddly feminine circumstance, not in a direct sense, but in the connection in my mind between male sex and female blood. Female blood was related to male sexual intrusion. Male blood was also related to sexuality, but sexuality intimately connected with violence. Blood had a passive and active character for me, a feminine and masculine role. Here I was, bleeding passively, like a woman.

One morning the bleeding would not stop. I cut my left hand, thinking a lesion there would relieve the pressure on my overworked nose. It didn't. I became terribly frightened. I stuffed cotton up my nose, which did not prevent the bleeding, because the blood only made a detour down my throat. I remember about six in the morning sitting in my reading chair, spitting blood into a bowl, and watching the sun flood in through the window and thinking I ought to jump. I was embarrassed by my body. If one is going to die, at least do it with some style, in the proper form.

I was, wouldn't you know it, unable to reach my doctor. I went downstairs and hailed a cab and went to Lenox Hill Hospital, where the bleeding was stopped for good.

When I returned to my studio I called Ruth, whom I love, and said I was scared to be alone anymore. I went and stayed with her. We never discussed what I was going through. She simply refused to let me out of her sight. I wanted to live. That was enough. In about a week I found myself writing again. I was home free.

I do not know what drove or enticed so many young people (mainly males) into self-destruction. I do not know that any more than I know why young people were caught up in the epidemic of hard drugs, or why they committed violence, or why they failed, or why they wanted to die, or why American society was so indifferent to their plight that its response to these young people, its sons, was confinement and enforcement of laws that were unjust and, worse, did not work. I know it had something to do with sexual disfigurement and dysfunction, with transgressions against, and mutilation of, young manhood, of a male's self-esteem. I know that because, to a greater or lesser degree, over the last seven and eight years I lived through and was intimate with many of the conditions and events that spoke of male disfigurement and despair. I was changed by it, injured in some lasting measure, and I suppose what remains of my life will be lived as an acting out of a course determined irrevocably by being witness and participant in an extraordinary era, a costly and dramatic one. Although my feelings about America are ambivalent (whose aren't? Outside the Joint Chiefs and the new Germans in the White House, whose feelings toward this brawling and deadly country are not split and contradictory and hurtful?), I believe I know the country well. I know something of its cities and the young men loose in them, the street boys and radicals and homosexuals and heads and blacks and beat-down hustlers, the outsiders. I still identify with them, as I do with the young prisoners of Walpole at play in their walled yard. I take their side. I am convinced that enormous, wrenching change must occur in America if more of the young are not to pay separately for collective, national failure. There are too many sons who believe too correctly that they have no place in America. That they are unwanted, excluded, orphaned here. The simple fact that most of these young people are poor and unskilled and often addicted and often violent, certainly unhappy, in no way diminishes the offense this country, its people, commits against them. Exclusion is the worst crime a collective can make against the young. It perverts the soul.

If I can be permitted a simple construction, I would say that if you are alive to what the nature of American society presently is, and if you are a writer serious about the function of your art, then it seems to me that you are required to constantly struggle to be outside, to avoid being enveloped by those who stand against your friends. But who are your friends? That is hard to know. That is something you have to continually work to know.

Listen again: I have learned one thing of importance to me—one has to act (write) against what is hurtful to one's friends. And its corollary: there is little one can do to much effect in any case.

The war is over. The prisoners have come home. And that is good and that is honorable, because peace is always honorable. But the war will not end in America, the combat between the classes and races and generations, until Reconstruction begins. And that is what I am waiting for.

A NOTE ON THE TYPE

This book was set on the Linotype in a face
called Primer, designed by Rudolph Ruzicka,
who was earlier responsible for the design
of Fairfield and Fairfield Medium, Linotype
faces whose virtues have for some time been
accorded wide recognition.

The complete range of sizes of Primer was
first made available in 1954, although the
pilot size of 12-point was ready as early as
1951. The design of the face makes general
reference to Linotype Century—long a
serviceable type, totally lacking in manner or
frills of any kind—but brilliantly corrects
its characterless quality.

This book was composed, printed, and bound
by The Book Press, Brattleboro, Vermont.
Typography and binding design by
Susan Mitchell.